The
GREEK YOGURT
Cookbook

Lauren Kelly, CN

Includes over 125 delicious, nutritious Greek yogurt recipes

adamsmedia
Avon, Massachusetts

I dedicate this book to my husband, Steve, and my three amazing children.
Without all of your help "taste-tasting," this book just wouldn't be the same.
I love you!

Published by
Adams Media, a division of F+W Media, Inc.
57 Littlefield Street, Avon, MA 02322. U.S.A.
www.adamsmedia.com

ISBN 10: 1-4405-6736-0
ISBN 13: 978-1-4405-6736-0
eISBN 10: 1-4405-6737-9
eISBN 13: 978-1-4405-6737-7

Printed in the United States of America.

10 9 8 7 6 5 4 3 2 1

Always follow safety and commonsense cooking protocol while using kitchen utensils, operating ovens and stoves, and handling uncooked food. If children are assisting in the preparation of any recipe, they should always be supervised by an adult.

Many of the designations used by manufacturers and sellers to distinguish their product are claimed as trademarks. Where those designations appear in this book and F+W Media was aware of a trademark claim, the designations have been printed with initial capital letters.

Photos courtesy of Sylvia McArdle.

Cover image © 123rf.com.

This book is available at quantity discounts for bulk purchases.
For information, please call 1-800-289-0963.

Acknowledgments

Thank you to all of my friends and family for their support and encouragement. You make me feel like there is nothing I can't do. Thank you to my wonderful husband for everything you did to make this possible. Thank you to all of my incredible friends who stuck by me during this process. Thank you Dad for your support and for being so proud of me. Mom, I know you are smiling down on me. Thanks again for teaching me to cook! Can you believe I wrote another cookbook?

I would also like to thank my agent, Joelle Delbourgo, for her guidance and assistance. You are the best! Finally, thank you to my editor, Ross Weisman, who was a dream to work with, and all of the fantastic people at Adams Media.

CONTENTS

Chapter 4

SMOOTHIES

Chapter 5

ENTRÉES

Chapter 6

SIDE DISHES

INTRODUCTION

Greek yogurt's popularity has skyrocketed in the past few years, and for good reason. In addition to containing the calcium and protein your body needs, it has an unforgettable tangy taste and an irresistible, velvety texture. You may have tried Greek yogurt—perhaps you regularly indulge in this cool, creamy treat for breakfast or as an alternative to your regular flavored yogurt. But its use doesn't have to be limited to traditional Mediterranean cuisine or an occasional healthy snack. *The Greek Yogurt Cookbook* delivers over 125 flavor-packed recipes that show you how to make Greek yogurt a kitchen essential, whether it's swirled up in smoothies, stirred into soups, or adding depth of flavor to your main courses.

As a nutritionist, I not only eat Greek yogurt every day, but I recommend it to my clients as well. I have been eating yogurt for as long as I can remember. From the time I was a little girl, eating a small snack cup of strawberry yogurt in my lunch box, to my adult cravings for Greek yogurt as a late-night snack, yogurt has been a go-to staple as a part of a healthy diet. With this complete resource, you too can have all the benefits of yogurt—and satisfy your cravings in creative, wholesome ways.

Yogurt, most commonly made from cow's milk (although there are varieties made from sheep's and goat's milk, as well as soy), is popular in many countries throughout the world.

Yogurt is a dairy product created from live bacteria in milk, also known as "cultures." But what is the difference between regular yogurt and Greek yogurt? While both can be part of a healthy diet, Greek yogurt does have a significant advantage. Greek yogurt goes through an extra straining process that removes the excess sugars and liquids found in traditional yogurt, leaving the yogurt much thicker. Greek yogurt not only contains much more protein than regular yogurt, it also has a much creamier texture and less sugar. A typical 6-ounce cup of plain Greek yogurt contains roughly 15–20 grams of protein, which is the equivalent of 3 eggs, 2–3 ounces of chicken breast, or 12 ounces of regular yogurt.

Protein is a vital part of every cell in your body. It is necessary for building and maintaining muscles, forming tissues and cells, and strengthening bones, skin, and blood. Eating foods high in protein, like Greek yogurt, also helps to keep you full for longer amounts of time. If you're a vegetarian, adding Greek yogurt to your diet will help your body get the protein it needs for optimal health. There are many vegetarian recipes throughout this cookbook for you to enjoy—just look for the Ⓥ symbol!

Greek yogurt is loaded with calcium, a mineral that is essential for maintaining optimum health. Calcium keeps your teeth and bones strong and healthy, and it also helps keep your heart and nerves functioning properly. In addition to calcium, Greek yogurt is packed with live active cultures. These cultures, called probiotics, improve your overall digestive health. They keep the "good" bacteria in your gut healthy, and can improve your entire immune system. Look for "contains live and active cultures" on the label of your Greek yogurt container.

The delicious recipes in this book will show you that Greek yogurt's popularity is more than just a fleeting food trend; its adaptability, unique flavor, and smooth texture will make it a staple for all cooking styles. If you are looking for a healthier and tastier way to add protein to some of your favorite dishes, let *The Greek Yogurt Cookbook* be your guide.

Chapter 1

YOUR ESSENTIAL GUIDE TO GREEK YOGURT

Yogurt is considered to be one of the oldest foods in history. Some historians think yogurt was around as far back as 9000 B.C. It is believed that yogurt may have been discovered accidentally by earlier civilizations trying to store milk in warm climates. This began the fermentation process of the milk, resulting in what we now know as yogurt. It is thought to have originated in the Middle East, and traditionally it is called Greek yogurt.

In the United States in the mid-twentieth century, there was a major shift toward greater health consciousness and more wholesome foods. As a result of this increasing health food craze in the 1950s and 1960s, yogurt's popularity also increased. Americans began adding more and more yogurt to their weekly grocery lists. This increase in demand can be directly attributed to its health benefits, convenience, and taste. Today, yogurt is a common staple in American diets.

Skyrocketing Sales

According to Packagefacts.com, annual sales of Greek yogurt rose to an approximate $1.5 billion in 2012. Sales are projected to reach an astounding $9.3 billion by 2017. That is an incredible increase in sales, and there are many good reasons why!

Practically unknown just a few years ago, Greek yogurt has become the fashionable snack of choice. Greek yogurt has replaced the other more traditional varieties of yogurt due to its increased health benefits and thicker, creamier texture. For price comparison purposes, consider these facts: 1 cup of milk equals 1 cup of regular yogurt. Because Greek yogurt is strained so many times, it takes more milk to create 1 cup of yogurt. This is the reason why Greek yogurt may be a little more expensive than traditional yogurt, but most health experts agree that the extra cost is worth the nutritional benefits you'll receive.

HEALTH BENEFITS

Greek yogurt is packed with vitamins, minerals, protein, and important probiotic cultures. One serving of Greek yogurt is a well-balanced breakfast or snack, and can be used as a healthy addition to many of your favorite recipes. The main reason that Greek yogurt has become increasingly popular is its health benefits.

A HIGH-PROTEIN FOOD

Greek yogurt is loaded with protein. A 6-ounce container of plain Greek yogurt contains approximately 15–20 grams of protein. That's a great deal of protein in a small serving size.

This is particularly encouraging for vegetarians who do not eat meat and therefore may struggle to eat enough protein on a daily basis. Many of the common high-protein sources are found in red meat, chicken, and fish, thus making it challenging to follow a vegetarian diet. Eating Greek yogurt is a great way for vegetarians to supplement their protein. Greek yogurt is also a great post-workout snack, as the protein is essential for muscle growth and recovery.

One very important aspect of protein is that it helps keep you full for a longer amount of time. Eating more protein may even help you lose weight. Nutritionists often tell clients to make sure that they are eating some form of protein in every snack and meal they have. High-protein diets have become increasingly popular over the past ten years, but proceed with caution, as consuming too much protein is not good for your body.

RECOMMENDED DIETARY ALLOWANCE FOR PROTEIN	
Age	Grams of Protein Needed Each Day
Children ages 1–3	13
Children ages 4–8	19
Children ages 9–13	34
Girls ages 14–18	46
Boys ages 14–18	52
Women ages 19–70+	46
Men ages 19–70+	56

Data provided by CDC/National Academies Press (www.nap.edu)

According to the Centers for Disease Control and Prevention (CDC), it is recommended that 10–35 percent of your daily caloric intake come from protein. Many people do not eat enough protein and are not aware of how much protein their bodies require. The preceding chart from the CDC details the recommended amounts of protein for consumers of all ages. Use it as a guideline for your own protein intake, as well as that of your family or those you care for.

CARBOHYDRATES AND SUGARS

Plain Greek yogurt is also low in carbohydrates and sugars. Greek yogurt goes through an extra straining process through a cheesecloth where much of the milk sugar, also known as lactose, is removed. This not only creates a thicker, creamier yogurt, but also one that is much lower in carbohydrates, sugar, and lactose. This is desirable for those who are lactose-intolerant—they may find it easier to digest Greek yogurt compared to regular yogurt. Be careful when choosing your brand of Greek yogurt. Many of the flavored Greek yogurts have added sugars and calories. Read your labels carefully, and choose a flavored Greek yogurt with a lower sugar content, with preferably no more than 20 grams of sugar per serving. Better yet, stick to plain Greek yogurt, which has only 7 grams of sugar (all from natural lactose) and top it with fresh fruit, which adds natural sweetness.

CALCIUM AND LIVE CULTURES

Greek yogurt is also a great source of calcium. A 6-ounce cup of plain Greek yogurt contains approximately 20 percent of the daily recommended requirement for calcium. Calcium is an essential mineral that is crucial for bone and teeth growth, and may help with regulating blood pressure.

Greek yogurt also contains live cultures, which are important probiotics (healthy bacteria) that have shown to be crucial in maintaining proper digestive and overall health. There are many factors that may disturb the balance of these bacteria growing in the digestive tracts of our bodies. Stress, diet, and the use of antibiotics are a few ways your equilibrium can become unsettled. The probiotics found in Greek yogurt help to retain the balance in your body. Doctors and nutritionists recommend consuming additional live cultures to maintain a healthy digestive tract, and doctors often prescribe consuming yogurt alongside antibiotics. Many Greek yogurt labels will not only state that they contain live cultures, but they will list them in the ingredient list. This "good" bacteria aids in the digestion of your foods, and boosts your overall immune system.

KEY FACTORS FOR SELECTING YOGURT

Another important factor to consider when choosing a type of Greek yogurt is their varying fat contents. The fat content can range from 0 percent fat, to low fat, to varieties that are full-fat and made with whole milk. According to *http://health.usnews.com*, one 8-ounce serving of full-fat Greek yogurt can contain as much as 5–17 grams of saturated fat. Saturated fat increases the "bad" cholesterol and should be limited, especially for those who run the risk of heart disease. One serving won't hurt you, but be conscious of this aspect if you are eating full-fat Greek yogurt on a regular basis. If you're concerned about the fat content in full-fat yogurt, try switching to low-fat or nonfat varieties.

Are You Watching Your Sodium Intake?

Besides containing more protein than regular yogurt, Greek yogurt has less sodium. Much of the sodium is removed in the straining process, leaving Greek yogurt with about half the sodium of ordinary yogurt. Too much sodium in your diet can increase your risk of high blood pressure.

Read your labels carefully. It should say "Greek Yogurt" and not "Greek-Style Yogurt." Greek-style yogurt may be regular-style yogurt with added thickening agents such as gelatin, milk protein concentrates, or cornstarch. True Greek yogurt will not contain any of these thickening agents; it will be naturally thick and creamy on its own. These thickening agents are just extra additives and make the Greek-style yogurt a more processed food.

VERSATILITY

With its creamy texture and mild taste, Greek yogurt is often substituted for many unhealthier ingredients, such as sour cream, buttermilk, butter, cream cheese, oil, heavy cream, and mayonnaise. Greek yogurt can replace these items in salad dressings, baked goods, sauces, dips, desserts, and more. Adding Greek yogurt to these meals is a wonderful way to save calories and add protein to your favorite dishes.

Chobani has created this easy conversion chart to help you substitute plain Greek yogurt in your favorite recipes:

1 cup butter = ¼ cup Greek yogurt + ½ cup butter	
1 cup oil = ¾ cup Greek yogurt	
1 cup sour cream = 1 cup Greek yogurt	
1 cup mayonnaise = 1 cup Greek yogurt	
1 cup cream cheese = 1 cup Greek yogurt	
1 cup buttermilk = ⅔ cup Greek yogurt + ⅓ cup milk or buttermilk	
1 cup heavy cream = ½ cup Greek yogurt + ½ cup heavy cream	
1 cup milk = ¼ cup Greek yogurt + ¾ cup milk	
1 cup crème fraîche = 1 cup Greek yogurt	

(www.chobani.com)

Since Greek yogurt has the same appearance and creamy texture as sour cream, it makes a healthy substitution for those toppings on your favorite Mexican dishes. One tablespoon of plain 0 percent Fage Greek yogurt has a mere 8 calories, whereas 1 tablespoon of regular sour cream has 30 calories; even "light" sour cream has 22 calories per tablespoon. This is not a considerable difference when just using a tablespoon, but those calories can add up when you are consuming more.

ADD IT TO YOUR FAVORITE RECIPES

Greek yogurt works wonderfully in many recipes, both sweet and savory. Greek yogurt is a wonderful way to add creaminess to soups and sauces without all the extra fat and calories. It makes a wonderful marinade for meats because it adds flavor and moisture while also tenderizing the meat. When cooking food over a stove, be sure to remove it from the heat before adding the Greek yogurt. By removing it from the heat first, you will prevent the Greek yogurt from curdling and also preserve the beneficial bacteria that would have been removed when directly heated. Make sure to stir continuously to prevent sticking.

Sip Smoothies!

Smoothies are also an easy and convenient way to add calcium to your diet. The beauty of plain Greek yogurt is that it goes nicely with any flavor smoothie. Its creamy texture adds thickness along with all the nutritious benefits. Simply adding 6 ounces of Greek yogurt to your juice or smoothie increases the protein content, which in turn helps to keep you full.

GREEK YOGURT FOR BAKING

Baking with Greek yogurt is ideal. It adds creaminess and protein and can reduce the fat and calories in many of your favorite cakes, cookies, and muffins. One thing to be aware of is that Greek yogurt contains less liquid than milk and buttermilk, so you may have to add a little extra liquid to the batter. This "liquid" can be some more Greek yogurt, or maybe a little water or applesauce to make it a little thinner. Be careful not to overmix when baking with Greek yogurt. It is recommended that you fold the Greek yogurt in to blend it in with other ingredients. Be careful when baking, however; the acidity in Greek yogurt may react with aluminum cookware or bakeware, and it may change the flavor of your foods. You should avoid baking with aluminum cookware when using Greek yogurt.

CHOOSING GREEK YOGURT FOR LIFE

With the many brands of Greek yogurt available in grocery stores these days, you may feel a bit overwhelmed when choosing a brand that's right for you. The key solution is simple: Always read nutrition labels to make sure your yogurt meets your needs. Take a quick stroll down the dairy aisle, and you'll find many different flavors and brands of Greek yogurt. All varieties have different nutritional information, and it is essential for you to read the labels, to make sure the brands and flavors you're buying stay within your dietary guidelines. With so many to choose from, you're bound to find the perfect Greek yogurt for you!

The Greek yogurt "fad" is here to stay. A food that is delicious, healthy, and such a versatile ingredient in so many different recipes truly is a "superfood." Adding more Greek yogurt to your diet will help you feel healthier. Greek yogurt has the perfect balance of protein, carbohydrates, and fat that keeps your blood sugar level. Greek yogurt can easily replace many ingredients that are loaded with extra fat in many of your favorite recipes. But don't worry—your recipes will still taste delicious! So experiment with substituting Greek yogurt into some of your favorite recipes, try the recipes in this cookbook, and see for yourself just how wonderful Greek yogurt is. Here's to many years of happy and healthy eating. *Bon appétit!*

Chapter 2

BREAKFAST AND BRUNCH

Your parents were right: Breakfast really is the most important meal of the day. It is also very important for your breakfast to include protein, because protein keeps your mind sharp and focused and helps to keep you feeling full. It is crucial that children consume protein at breakfast to help them remain attentive in school. In addition, many people don't make time for breakfast in the morning, and feel sluggish and ravenous by mid-morning. Studies show that those who skip breakfast tend to eat more over the course of the day. If you are trying to watch your weight, it is beneficial to take the time to eat a nutritious breakfast and to avoid overeating those midday snacks. Adding Greek yogurt to your favorite breakfast and brunch dishes each day will ensure that you get a healthy start, and ensure that your body gets the protein it needs to power you through the day.

In this chapter, you will find many creative recipes that can be fixed ahead of time, making them perfect for those hectic mornings. Planning ahead takes the guesswork out of having to cook that healthy breakfast for the family when time is limited. This chapter contains many unique, delicious, and nutritious options for a well-balanced, healthy breakfast.

Green Tea Quinoa Muffins

These muffins are packed with healthy ingredients. Both chia seeds and flaxseeds are full of omega-3 fatty acids and fiber. Green tea is loaded with antioxidants, and the quinoa and Greek yogurt add protein. Who says muffins can't be healthy?

Ⓥ YIELDS 12 MUFFINS

Ingredients

¼ cup cooked quinoa

½ cup whole-wheat pastry flour

½ cup ground flaxseed (or flax meal)

1 tablespoon ground chia seeds

1 teaspoon baking powder

1 teaspoon salt

2 teaspoons green tea matcha powder

½ cup packed brown sugar

1 teaspoon pure vanilla extract

3 tablespoons melted unsalted organic butter

½ cup nonfat plain Greek yogurt

2 ripe, mashed bananas

PER MUFFIN

Calories: 135	Sugar: 9 g
Fat: 5 g	Fiber: 3 g
Cholesterol: 8 mg	Sodium: 244 mg
Carbohydrates: 21 g	Protein: 3 g

1. Preheat the oven to 400°F. Grease muffin tins or use cupcake liners. Set aside cooked quinoa and allow to cool.
2. Combine flour, ground flax, chia seeds, baking powder, salt, and green tea matcha powder in a medium bowl. Add cooled, cooked quinoa and stir to combine. Set aside.
3. In another medium bowl, mix brown sugar, vanilla, butter, Greek yogurt, and bananas.
4. Add the sugar mixture to the flour mixture and stir to combine, being careful not to overmix. Place into greased muffin tins.
5. Bake for 25–30 minutes for regular-size muffins, and 12–15 minutes for mini muffins, or until a toothpick inserted into the center of a muffin comes out clean. Allow muffins to cool in the pan.
6. Serve immediately, or store in an airtight container in the refrigerator for up to 5 days.

Strawberry Banana Bread

Turbinado sugar is less processed, which allows it to retain some nutrients that ordinary white sugar does not have. The mashed bananas and Greek yogurt in this bread add extra moisture.

V SERVES 8

Ingredients

1½ cups whole-wheat pastry flour
1½ teaspoons baking powder
½ teaspoon kosher salt
3 large ripe bananas
2 eggs
4 tablespoons turbinado sugar
½ cup honey
¾ cup low-fat plain Greek yogurt
1 cup diced strawberries

PER SERVING (PER SLICE)

Calories: 258
Fat: 2.5 g
Cholesterol: 54 mg
Carbohydrates: 54.5 g

Sugar: 26 g
Fiber: 4 g
Sodium: 288 mg
Protein: 6.75 g

1. Preheat the oven to 375°F. Combine flour, baking powder, and salt in a large mixing bowl.
2. In a separate bowl, mash bananas with a fork until they are almost like a liquid.
3. Add eggs, sugar, and honey to the bananas, and mix thoroughly. Next, add the Greek yogurt. Whisk until everything is well combined and there are no lumps.
4. Pour the wet ingredients into the dry ingredients, and mix until just combined. Next, fold in the fresh strawberries. Pour the batter into 4 (5½" × 3") mini loaf pans (sprayed with organic nonstick cooking spray). You could also use 1 (9" × 5") loaf pan, but adjust the cooking time to 40 minutes.
5. Bake for 35 minutes, or until the top is golden brown and a toothpick comes out clean.
6. Transfer to a cooling rack and allow the bread to cool for at least 10 minutes before slicing.

Applesauce Carrot Spice Muffins

Butter isn't necessary in these healthy muffins—and you won't even know it's missing. The applesauce and Greek yogurt make wonderful substitutions!

YIELDS 12 MUFFINS

Ingredients

Dry Ingredients
1¾ cups whole-wheat flour
¼ cup turbinado sugar
2 tablespoons ground flaxseed
1 teaspoon baking powder
1 teaspoon baking soda
1 teaspoon cinnamon
¾ teaspoon ground ginger
⅛ teaspoon cloves
½ teaspoon salt

Wet Ingredients
⅓ cup honey
⅓ cup unsweetened applesauce
½ cup nonfat plain Greek yogurt
¼ cup water
1 teaspoon pure vanilla extract
1½ cups shredded carrots (about 3 carrots)
¼ cup raisins (optional)

PER SERVING (PER MUFFIN,
WITH RAISINS)

Calories: 138	Sugar: 15 g
Fat: 0.8 g	Fiber: 3.4 g
Cholesterol: 0 mg	Sodium: 259 mg
Carbohydrates: 31 g	Protein: 4 g

1. Preheat the oven to 400°F. Spray a muffin pan with organic nonstick cooking spray or use muffin liners.
2. Mix together all dry ingredients in a large bowl. In a small bowl, combine the wet ingredients. Add all wet ingredients except carrots and raisins to the dry, and mix just long enough to combine. Fold in the carrots and raisins until combined.
3. Spoon the batter into the muffin cups. The mixture will be very thick. Bake for 15–20 minutes, until a toothpick comes out clean when inserted in the center of a muffin.

DELIGHTFUL LEMON BERRY SCONES

Don't be intimidated by the prospect of making scones. These are not only simple to make, but they're also delicious and incredibly healthy. The whole-wheat flour adds fiber, and the milk and Greek yogurt add protein. With only 3 tablespoons of butter in the entire recipe, how can you go wrong?

 YIELDS 8 SCONES

Ingredients

1½ cups whole-wheat pastry flour

½ cup whole-wheat flour

1 tablespoon baking powder

3 tablespoons turbinado sugar, plus more for sprinkling on top

⅛ teaspoon salt

3 tablespoons cold unsalted butter

¾ cup dried berries

¼ teaspoon natural lemon extract

Zest of 1 lemon

½ cup nonfat plain Greek yogurt

½ cup low-fat milk

PER SCONE

Calories: 218	Sugar: 13 g
Fat: 5.25 g	Fiber: 4.5 g
Cholesterol: 13 mg	Sodium: 235 mg
Carbohydrates: 39 g	Protein: 5.4 g

1. Preheat the oven to 425°F.
2. Combine the flours, baking powder, sugar, and salt in a medium bowl and whisk together.
3. Slice the butter into small pieces and drop into dry ingredients. Mix sliced butter into the flour mixture. The mixture should have clumps.
4. Add dried berries, lemon extract, and lemon zest and gently stir.
5. Gently mix in Greek yogurt and milk. Eventually you'll need to use your hands to knead the last of the flour into the dough. Since a small amount of butter is used in this recipe, you really have to work with your hands to make sure all the ingredients are mixed.
6. Form the dough into a circle that's about 1" deep all around. Cut the circle into 8 slices.
7. Separate the slices and place on a baking sheet covered in parchment paper or foil.
8. Sprinkle the tops of the scones with a bit of turbinado sugar.
9. Bake for 15 minutes or until the scones are light brown and puffed.

OVERNIGHT PEANUT BUTTER BANANA OATMEAL

Why not make your breakfast the night before, and save yourself some time in the morning? Prepare all of the ingredients (except the peanut butter) the night before, and place in a covered dish in the refrigerator. In the morning, simply stir in the peanut butter and bake!

 SERVES 8

Ingredients

Dry Ingredients
2 cups oats
½ teaspoon ground cinnamon
¼ teaspoon baking soda
½ teaspoon baking powder
¼ cup ground flaxseed

Wet Ingredients
2 sliced ripe bananas
1 cup unsweetened almond milk
¾ cup nonfat plain Greek yogurt
1 large egg, lightly beaten
¼ cup 100 percent pure maple syrup
¼ cup natural peanut butter

1. Prepare a 1.5-quart baking dish with organic nonstick cooking spray.
2. Mix all dry ingredients together in a medium bowl. Set aside.
3. Mix all wet ingredients together in a separate medium bowl. Then add the wet ingredients to the dry and mix well. Pour the mixture into the prepared baking dish. Cover with a lid and place in the refrigerator.
4. In the morning, preheat the oven to 350°F. Bake for 30 minutes until the top is golden brown. Let cool for a few minutes before serving.

PER SERVING

Calories: 309	Sugar: 9 g
Fat: 9.25 g	Fiber: 6 g
Cholesterol: 26 mg	Sodium: 149 mg
Carbohydrates: 45 g	Protein: 12.5 g

SINFULLY DELICIOUS CINNAMON ROLLS

Make these the night before and they will be ready to bake in the morning. Your kitchen will smell delightful and your family will thank you. Typical cinnamon rolls are loaded with fat and calories, and include a large list of ingredients. These are simple to make and have much less sugar than average cinnamon rolls.

Ⓥ YIELDS 24 CINNAMON ROLLS

Ingredients

2 packages active dry yeast

¼ cup warm water

1½ cups nonfat plain Greek yogurt, at room temperature

1 cup unsalted melted butter, divided use

2½ cups all-purpose flour

2 cups whole-wheat pastry flour

1 teaspoon salt

1¼ cups packed brown sugar

2 teaspoons ground cinnamon

PER ROLL

Calories: 207	Sugar: 12 g
Fat: 8 g	Fiber: 2 g
Cholesterol: 20 mg	Sodium: 110 mg
Carbohydrates: 30 g	Protein: 4 g

1. In a large bowl, dissolve yeast packets in warm water. Let sit for about 10 minutes, until the consistency is creamy.
2. Pour the Greek yogurt and ½ cup melted butter into the yeast. Mix well and set aside.
3. In a separate large bowl, combine flours and salt. Slowly pour the flour mixture into the yeast combination until a soft dough forms. Knead the dough for 7–8 minutes until it is smooth and stretchy. Cover and let sit for 1 hour to allow dough to rise.
4. In a small bowl, combine ½ cup melted butter, brown sugar, and cinnamon. Prepare 2 large baking sheets with butter and flour by lightly spreading butter onto the baking sheets, and coating with flour.
5. After dough has risen, lightly flour your work surface and roll out the dough into a large rectangle. Spread the cinnamon mixture all over the dough. Let sit for a few minutes to cool.
6. Roll up the dough from the longest side, making it as tightly rolled together as possible, and pinch edges together to seal. Slice into 1" slices and place on the prepared baking sheets. Let sit to rise again for approximately 1 hour. You can refrigerate these overnight or bake immediately. When baking, preheat the oven to 375°F. Bake for 25 minutes, until browned.

ARTICHOKE MUSHROOM GRUYÈRE CRUSTLESS QUICHE

This light and airy quiche makes the perfect addition to any brunch. You won't miss the crust in this scrumptious recipe.

 SERVES 8

Ingredients
1 tablespoon grapeseed oil
1 cup sliced artichoke hearts
1 cup cleaned, sliced baby bella mushrooms
3 whole eggs
1 cup nonfat plain Greek yogurt
¼ cup shredded Gruyère cheese

PER SERVING

Calories: 99	Sugar: 3 g
Fat: 5.5 g	Fiber: 0 g
Cholesterol: 83 mg	Sodium: 89 mg
Carbohydrates: 5.25 g	Protein: 7 g

1. Preheat the oven to 375°F. Spray a 8" or 9" casserole dish or pie plate with organic nonstick cooking spray.
2. Heat the grapeseed oil in a medium sauté pan over medium-high heat. When the oil is hot, place artichoke hearts and mushrooms in pan and sauté for 4–5 minutes until soft.
3. Place the artichokes and mushrooms in the bottom of the sprayed casserole dish or pie plate.
4. In a large bowl, add eggs and Greek yogurt, and beat until frothy. Pour into the casserole dish or pie plate on top of the vegetables.
5. Sprinkle with shredded cheese. Bake for 35 minutes or until the top is set and the edges are golden brown.

OATMEAL PANCAKES

Who says pancakes are just for breakfast? These are so light and fluffy, you will want to eat them all day long. Pancakes made from a box are overly processed and filled with preservatives that aren't good for you. These are made healthier by using only 1 teaspoon of sugar and no butter at all.

 YIELDS 15 PANCAKES

Ingredients

1 cup low-fat milk

1 cup nonfat vanilla Greek yogurt

2 eggs

1 cup whole-wheat flour

1 cup oats

1 teaspoon turbinado sugar

1 teaspoon baking powder

½ teaspoon baking soda

¼ teaspoon salt

½ teaspoon ground cinnamon

1 teaspoon 100 percent pure maple syrup

PER PANCAKE

Calories: 101	Sugar: 1 g
Fat: 2 g	Fiber: 2 g
Cholesterol: 29 mg	Sodium: 152 mg
Carbohydrates: 15 g	Protein: 6 g

1. In a medium bowl, mix milk, Greek yogurt, and eggs until smooth.
2. Add flour, oats, sugar, baking powder, baking soda, salt, cinnamon, and syrup. Mix well until thoroughly combined.
3. Coat a large skillet with organic nonstick cooking spray or butter and place over medium heat. Pour batter onto skillet to form pancakes, and cook each side until small bubbles form, about 1 minute each side. Continue to cook until all batter is used. Serve immediately with maple syrup and butter if desired.

Add Nutrition to Your Pancakes!

Looking to add some fiber, antioxidants, and omega-3 fatty acids to your pancakes? Substitute ¼ of the flour with ground flaxseed, also known as flax meal. You won't even taste the flax, but you will get added nutrition. The omega-3 fatty acids help fight inflammation in the body and help prevent certain diseases. Ground flax can be found in most supermarkets.

BAKED APPLESAUCE DOUGHNUTS

You don't have to feel guilty about eating doughnuts anymore! These are baked, not fried. If you don't have a doughnut pan, you can easily use a regular-size muffin tin instead.

 YIELDS 24 DOUGHNUTS

Ingredients

¼ cup butter, at room temperature
½ cup turbinado sugar
⅓ cup packed brown sugar
1 large egg
1½ teaspoons baking powder
¼ teaspoon baking soda
1 teaspoon ground cinnamon
⅔ cup oats
1 cup whole-wheat pastry flour
⅓ cup low-fat milk
1 cup nonfat vanilla Greek yogurt
½ cup applesauce, unsweetened
1 cup all-purpose flour

PER DOUGHNUT

Calories: 117	Sugar: 8 g
Fat: 2.75 g	Fiber: 1.5 g
Cholesterol: 14 mg	Sodium: 72 mg
Carbohydrates: 20 g	Protein: 3 g

1. Preheat the oven to 425°F. Grease the doughnut pan or muffin tin.
2. In a large bowl, cream together the butter, sugars, and egg until smooth, about 5 minutes with electric mixer on medium-high setting.
3. Mix in the baking powder, baking soda, cinnamon, and oats to the creamed mixture. Mix thoroughly, making sure to scrape the sides.
4. On low speed, add the whole-wheat pastry flour and milk. Mix well. Add the Greek yogurt, applesauce, and all-purpose flour. Mix until combined, being careful not to overmix.
5. Fill the prepared doughnut pan or muffin tin and bake for 12–15 minutes. Let cool in the pan for a few minutes, then place on wire rack for 5 minutes to cool before adding a glaze. Try glazing with Vanilla Yogurt Glaze (see recipe in this chapter).

Vanilla Yogurt Glaze

So simple, this glaze can be used for a variety of baked goods. Greek yogurt adds the perfect amount of thickness (and protein) to create this delicious glaze.

 YIELDS 1 CUP

Ingredients
½ cup nonfat vanilla Greek yogurt
¾ cup powdered sugar

PER TABLESPOON

Calories: 28	Sugar: 6 g
Fat: 0 g	Fiber: 0 g
Cholesterol: 0 mg	Sodium: 3 mg
Carbohydrates: 6 g	Protein: 0.7 g

In a small bowl, mix ingredients well. Allow to thicken in the refrigerator for 10 minutes before applying to a doughnut (or other baked good).

Amazing Apple Cinnamon Quinoa

Quinoa is a seed that is a complete protein on its own—it contains all the essential amino acids your body needs. With its texture and appearance similar to oatmeal, you won't believe you are eating quinoa!

 SERVES 4

Ingredients

3½ cups water

1⅓ cups quinoa flakes

½ cup nonfat plain Greek yogurt

½ teaspoon ground cinnamon

1 apple, diced

3 tablespoons 100 percent pure maple syrup

4 tablespoons sliced almonds

Cinnamon, for topping

PER SERVING

Calories: 339	Sugar: 10.25 g
Fat: 8.25 g	Fiber: 6.25 g
Cholesterol: 1.25 mg	Sodium: 17 mg
Carbohydrates: 55.25 g	Protein: 13 g

1. Place water in a large saucepan on the stove and bring to a rapid boil.
2. Add quinoa flakes and continue to boil for 1½ minutes, stirring frequently.
3. Remove from heat. Add Greek yogurt, cinnamon, apple, and maple syrup; mix thoroughly.
4. Top with sliced almonds (1 tablespoon per serving) and extra cinnamon if desired.

GLUTEN-FREE CHOCOLATE CHIP ZUCCHINI BREAD

The texture of this bread is fantastic—you'd never know it doesn't contain gluten. Get creative and substitute any fruit you'd like for the chocolate chips in this bread, or try adding chopped nuts for extra protein. The possibilities are endless!

 SERVES 8

Ingredients

2 eggs

½ cup turbinado sugar

½ cup grapeseed oil

½ cup nonfat vanilla Greek yogurt

½ teaspoon gluten-free vanilla extract

1 cup brown rice flour

½ cup almond flour

½ cup cornstarch

1 teaspoon xanthan gum

½ teaspoon gluten-free baking soda

¼ teaspoon gluten-free baking powder

½ teaspoon salt

1 tablespoon ground cinnamon

¼ teaspoon ground cloves

¼ teaspoon nutmeg

¼ cup ground flaxseed (optional)

1½ cups shredded fresh zucchini

½ cup chocolate chips

1. Preheat the oven to 350°F. Grease a 9" × 5" loaf pan with organic nonstick cooking spray.
2. In a large mixing bowl, beat together the eggs, sugar, oil, and Greek yogurt. Add the vanilla and mix well.
3. In a separate bowl, combine the flours, cornstarch, xanthan gum, baking soda, baking powder, salt, cinnamon, cloves, nutmeg, and flaxseed (if using).
4. Add the dry ingredients to wet ingredients and mix well.
5. Add zucchini and chocolate chips and stir to combine.
6. Pour into the greased loaf pan and bake for 60–70 minutes. Place a toothpick in the center of the bread; if it comes out clean, it's done.

Baking for Picky Eaters

If your kids won't eat vegetables, try this: Instead of shredding the zucchini, purée it in a blender. This way, the zucchini mixture won't be visible, and even your pickiest eaters won't suspect a thing.

PER SLICE, WITHOUT FLAXSEED

Calories: 438	Sugar: 23 g
Fat: 24 g	Fiber: 4.5 g
Cholesterol: 53 mg	Sodium: 293 mg
Carbohydrates: 52 g	Protein: 6.25 g

Greek Yogurt Parfait with Quinoa Granola

If you are looking for a quick, healthy breakfast, look no further. Most packaged granolas are marketed as "healthy" but instead are packed with extra fat, calories, and preservatives. This one is made with whole, healthy ingredients. You can make this granola ahead of time and store it in an airtight container for up to 5 days (if it lasts that long in your house!).

 YIELDS 4 CUPS GRANOLA

Ingredients

Quinoa Granola
1 cup organic whole-rolled oats
1 cup buckwheat groats
⅓ cup quinoa
¼ cup raw chopped walnuts
¾ cup raw chopped almonds
2 tablespoons ground chia seeds
¼ cup raw pumpkin seeds
¼ cup raw sunflower seeds
½ cup shredded coconut, unsweetened (optional)
2 teaspoons ground cinnamon
1 teaspoon ground ginger
1 teaspoon allspice
⅓ cup unsweetened dried cranberries (or other unsweetened fruit of your choice)
2 tablespoons chopped unsweetened apricots
⅓ cup chopped dates
½ cup 100 percent pure maple syrup
¼ cup organic coconut oil, melted

Parfait Assembly
1 cup plain nonfat or low-fat Greek yogurt
2 tablespoons Quinoa Granola
¼ cup fresh mixed berries and chopped fruit of your choice

1. To make the granola: Preheat the oven to 225°F. In a large bowl, mix the whole-rolled oats, buckwheat groats, and quinoa, then add the nuts, seeds, and coconut. Mix very well.
2. Add the cinnamon, ground ginger, and allspice; stir to combine. Fold in the cranberries, apricots, and dates until well incorporated.
3. Mix in the maple syrup and melted coconut oil. Make sure everything is mixed up and coated well.
4. Spoon and press the mixture onto a large baking sheet lined with waxed paper or parchment paper. Bake for 60 minutes.
5. Let cool after removing from oven, then pull the corners of waxed paper together to crumble granola.
6. To assemble the parfait: In a tall glass, spoon half the yogurt, 1 tablespoon granola, and half the fresh fruit. Repeat with a second layer of Greek yogurt, granola, and fruit. Serve immediately.

PER 1 PARFAIT, WITHOUT COCONUT

Calories: 272	Sugar: 16 g
Fat: 5.5 g	Fiber: 3.5 g
Cholesterol: 11 mg	Sodium: 82 mg
Carbohydrates: 29 g	Protein: 26 g

Vegetable Frittata

This frittata is so fluffy and flavorful, and is packed with protein from the Greek yogurt and eggs. It's a perfect, well-balanced dish for breakfast or brunch.

 SERVES 4

Ingredients

3 whole eggs

6 egg whites

½ cup nonfat plain Greek yogurt

¾ cup shredded Asiago cheese

1 tablespoon olive oil

1 garlic clove, minced

¼ cup minced onion

4 cups torn fresh spinach

½ cup chopped red bell pepper

1 cup sliced mushrooms

¼ teaspoon salt

¼ teaspoon ground pepper

1 tablespoon torn fresh basil

1 tablespoon grated Parmesan cheese

1. Preheat the broiler. In a large bowl, whisk together the eggs, egg whites, Greek yogurt, and Asiago cheese until well blended. Set aside.
2. Place olive oil in a medium ovenproof skillet along with garlic and onion. Cook over medium heat for 2–3 minutes until the onion becomes translucent.
3. Add spinach, red pepper, mushrooms, salt, pepper, and basil. Cook for 3–4 minutes until the vegetables soften.
4. Turn the heat to low and cover vegetables with the egg mixture. Cover, and cook on low heat for 5–7 minutes until the egg mixture is almost set.
5. Sprinkle Parmesan cheese on top of the egg mixture. Place the skillet under the broiler for 3–4 minutes until completely set. Let stand for 5 minutes before cutting into quarters. Serve immediately.

PER SERVING

Calories: 264

Fat: 16.5 g

Cholesterol: 183 mg

Carbohydrates: 6.5 g

Sugar: 3 g

Fiber: 1.5 g

Sodium: 700 mg

Protein: 21.5 g

HAM AND CHEDDAR BISCUITS

These flaky biscuits are perfect for brunch, or sliced in half to be used as bread for a sandwich. The ham and Cheddar give a nice, light flavor. Typical biscuits are filled with extra sugar, salt, and fat. The Greek yogurt not only adds protein, but it also replaces the butter or oil that other biscuits contain.

YIELDS 8 BISCUITS

Ingredients

2 cups all-purpose flour
½ teaspoon baking soda
1 teaspoon baking powder
½ teaspoon salt
1 cup nonfat plain Greek yogurt
½ cup low-fat milk
⅓ cup shredded Cheddar cheese
¼ cup diced ham

PER BISCUIT

Calories: 163	Sugar: 1 g
Fat: 2 g	Fiber: 1 g
Cholesterol: 9 mg	Sodium: 393 mg
Carbohydrates: 26 g	Protein: 9 g

1. Preheat the oven to 450°F. Line a baking sheet with parchment paper.
2. In a large bowl, mix the flour, baking soda, baking powder, and salt. Set aside.
3. In a small bowl, mix the Greek yogurt and milk until smooth. Pour the Greek yogurt mixture into the flour mixture and mix just until combined. Carefully fold in the Cheddar and diced ham. Do not overmix.
4. Flour your work surface and roll out the dough until it is 1" high. Cut out the biscuits using a biscuit cutter, making sure to reuse all the scraps to get more biscuits out of the dough.
5. Place biscuits onto the prepared baking sheet and bake for 20 minutes or until golden brown. Serve immediately.

Biscuit Tips

Don't have a biscuit cutter? Don't worry. You can easily use the band on a canning jar. You can also use a knife and cut them into squares.

OVERNIGHT FRENCH TOAST CASSEROLE

Your guests will be impressed when you serve this for brunch. You can easily make this the night before and bake it right before your guests arrive.

(V) SERVES 8

Ingredients

1 loaf stale bread
5 whole eggs
2 egg whites
1 cup nonfat vanilla Greek yogurt
1 cup low-fat milk
¾ cup 100 percent pure maple syrup
2 tablespoons cold butter, diced
⅓ cup brown sugar, packed
1 teaspoon ground cinnamon
¼ cup all-purpose flour
¼ cup minced pecans (optional)

PER SERVING, WITHOUT PECANS

Calories: 409	Sugar: 32 g
Fat: 10 g	Fiber: 1.6 g
Cholesterol: 142 mg	Sodium: 556 mg
	Protein: 13.5 g
Carbohydrates: 66 g	

1. Spray a 9" × 13" casserole dish with organic nonstick cooking spray.
2. Tear bread into pieces and spread them throughout the casserole dish in an even layer.
3. In a large bowl, mix eggs, egg whites, Greek yogurt, milk, and maple syrup. Mix very well until smooth and thoroughly combined. Pour egg mixture completely over bread.
4. In a small bowl, mix butter, brown sugar, cinnamon, flour, and pecans, if using. Mix until all ingredients are combined, even if still lumpy.
5. Sprinkle the butter mixture on top of the bread. Cover and refrigerate overnight. If cooking the same day, make sure to refrigerate at least 30 minutes before baking.
6. In the morning, preheat the oven to 350°F. Bake for 45 minutes until golden brown and the middle of the dish is set. Serve immediately with maple syrup, if desired.

Pear Muffins with Oatmeal Crunch Topping

My dear friend Robin created these delicious muffins, and she has really outdone herself! These muffins are light with a wonderful oatmeal topping. Robin blogs at Knead to Cook (*www.kneadtocook.com*).

Ⓥ YIELDS 12 MUFFINS

Ingredients

Muffins
¼ cup butter
½ cup turbinado sugar
2 eggs, at room temperature
¾ cup nonfat pear or plain Greek yogurt
1 cup all-purpose flour
1 cup whole-wheat flour
1 teaspoon baking soda
⅛ teaspoon salt
1 tablespoon ground flaxseed
2 pears, peeled and cored, finely chopped

Oatmeal Crunch Topping
1 tablespoon cold butter, cut into little cubes
¼ cup brown sugar
¼ cup all-purpose flour
¼ cup oats
¼ teaspoon ground cinnamon

1. Preheat the oven to 425°F. Spray a muffin pan with organic nonstick baking spray and set aside.
2. To make the muffins: Using an electric mixer, blend the butter with the sugar for 3–4 minutes, or until light and fluffy. Then add the eggs and Greek yogurt, and blend to combine.
3. In a separate bowl, blend the flours, baking soda, salt, and flax. Add the flour mixture to the mixer bowl. Add the pears, and blend until just combined.
4. Scoop the muffin mixture ¾ of the way full into each well.
5. To make the topping: In a medium bowl, add the cold butter pieces, brown sugar, flour, oats, and cinnamon. Blend with your hands, pinching the mixture until the butter is well incorporated. Then drop some on top of each muffin with your fingers. Bake for 12–14 minutes, or until they're golden brown and a toothpick inserted in the center comes out clean. Let cool in pan for a few minutes before transferring to wire rack to cool completely.

PER MUFFIN WITH TOPPING

Calories: 268	Sugar: 14 g
Fat: 11 g	Fiber: 2.8 g
Cholesterol: 59 mg	Sodium: 220 mg
Carbohydrates: 38 g	Protein: 6 g

Chapter 3

APPETIZERS

Having a dinner party is a great way to connect with friends and family. But before you sit down for that delicious meal, you need to stimulate your palate with some clever and delightful appetizers! Whether you're serving a light appetizer before a main course or featuring a range of hors d'oeuvres at a cocktail party, the recipes in this chapter are light and easy, and utilize Greek yogurt's adaptability and delicious flavor.

Appetizers should be quick and simple to make, not time-consuming—you don't want to be stuck in the kitchen while your guests are arriving. The recipes in this chapter allow you to create quick, irresistible, and healthy options for your family and friends. From rich, creamy soups to light, tangy dips, you won't have to sacrifice flavor to share nutritious, delicious appetizers. Greek yogurt is the perfect substitution for the typical unhealthy, high-calorie, and fat-laden options out there. Besides being high in protein and low in sugar, Greek yogurt adds a wonderful creamy texture to many dishes. Now you can indulge in your favorite snacks and treats without the guilt!

Summer Cucumber Soup

This refreshing light soup is perfect on a hot summer day. This recipe is simple to prepare, and should be made the night before to allow enough time for the ingredients to chill and the flavors to meld.

 SERVES 4

Ingredients

2 English cucumbers, peeled and chopped

2 cups reduced-fat buttermilk

1 cup nonfat plain Greek yogurt

2 teaspoons salt

Juice of 1 lemon

Rind of ½ lemon, minced

⅔ tablespoon snipped fresh dill weed

½ cup snipped fresh chives (snipped to ¼" pieces)

Freshly ground black pepper, to taste

Mix all ingredients in a nonreactive ceramic or porcelain bowl and blend together. Chill overnight. Serve in chilled bowls.

PER SERVING

Calories: 120

Fat: 2.75 g

Cholesterol: 12.5 mg

Carbohydrates: 12.25 g

Sugar: 10.25 g

Fiber: 1 g

Sodium: 1,291 mg

Protein: 11.75 g

Kale Artichoke Dip

This dip is great for entertaining, and is simple to prepare. Sliced vegetables are perfect with this creamy treat; serve sliced crudités on the side, or surrounding the dip on a big platter.

YIELDS 2 CUPS

Ingredients

1 (10-ounce) package chopped frozen kale, thawed

2 tablespoons extra-virgin olive oil

1 (12-ounce) jar artichoke hearts, drained and chopped

½ cup cream cheese, softened

1 cup nonfat plain Greek yogurt

2 cloves garlic, finely chopped

½ bunch scallions, chopped

2 tablespoons fresh lemon juice

¼ teaspoon freshly grated nutmeg

1 tablespoon shredded or grated Parmesan cheese

PER TABLESPOON

Calories: 34	Sugar: 0.3 g
Fat: 2.25 g	Fiber: 0.4 g
Cholesterol: 4.5 mg	Sodium: 28 mg
Carbohydrates: 2 g	Protein: 1.7 g

1. Drain the thawed kale and squeeze it with paper towels until the extra liquid is gone.
2. Heat the olive oil in a large skillet over medium heat. Add the kale; cook until just soft, about 5 minutes.
3. Remove the pan from the heat, and pour the kale into a large bowl. Add the rest of the ingredients to the bowl, stirring to mix.
4. To serve cold, place the mixture in a serving dish, and chill in the refrigerator until ready to serve. To serve warm, place the mixture in a small casserole dish and heat in the oven at 350°F for 7–10 minutes, until warmed through.

DEVILED EGGS

This classic appetizer is packed with protein. These are wonderful to bring to a party, and make a beautiful presentation.

 YIELDS 10 DEVILED EGGS

Ingredients
5 hard-boiled eggs

½ cup nonfat plain Greek yogurt

1 teaspoon Dijon mustard

1 teaspoon Tabasco sauce or other hot red pepper sauce

½ bunch of chives, finely snipped

2 teaspoons capers, the smallest available

Paprika, for garnish (optional)

PER SERVING

Calories: 46

Fat: 2.7 g

Cholesterol: 106.5 mg

Carbohydrates: 0.8 g

Sugar: 0.7 g

Fiber: 0 g

Sodium: 65 mg

Protein: 4.3 g

1. Peel eggs, cut them in half lengthwise, and remove the yolks. Add yolks to a food processor. Arrange the whites on a platter.
2. Add the Greek yogurt, mustard, Tabasco or pepper sauce, chives, and capers to the food processor, and process until blended.
3. Stuff the egg whites with the yolk mixture. Sprinkle with paprika, if desired, before serving.

TZATZIKI DIP

This Greek appetizer is the perfect complement to grilled meat or vegetables. Or you can serve it with baked pita chips as a healthy appetizer.

 SERVES 12

Ingredients

1 cup low-fat plain Greek yogurt
2 tablespoons extra-virgin olive oil
1 tablespoon lemon juice
½ teaspoon salt
½ teaspoon ground black pepper
1 tablespoon chopped fresh dill
2 garlic cloves, minced
2 tablespoons peeled, seeded, and minced English cucumber
1 tablespoon chopped fresh mint

PER SERVING

Calories: 36
Fat: 2.75 g
Cholesterol: 1 mg
Carbohydrates: 1.2 g

Sugar: 0.8 g
Fiber: 0 g
Sodium: 105 mg
Protein: 2 g

In a medium bowl, mix all the ingredients together until thoroughly combined. Refrigerate for at least 1 hour to let the flavors settle in. Serve cold with sliced raw vegetables, baked pita chips, or as a side to grilled meat.

A Mediterranean Treat

Tzatziki—pronounced tsah-ZEE-kee—is a Mediterranean sauce made with yogurt and cucumbers. It is traditionally served as a meze (an appetizer). This dip is low-carb and packed with high-quality protein.

GUACAMOLE

This guacamole has much less fat and many fewer calories than the typical version. Serve with your favorite chips, or use it to liven up a sandwich as a substitute for mayonnaise.

 YIELDS 2 CUPS

Ingredients

2 large ripe avocados, peeled and diced

1 tablespoon nonfat plain Greek yogurt

Juice of 2 limes

4 cloves garlic, finely minced

½ cup finely minced sweet onion

3 tablespoons salsa (or pico de gallo)

½ teaspoon Tabasco sauce, or to taste

½ teaspoon salt, or to taste

2 tablespoons finely chopped fresh cilantro

PER TABLESPOON

Calories: 26	Sugar: 0.7 g
Fat: 2 g	Fiber: 1.2 g
Cholesterol: 0 mg	Sodium: 44 mg
Carbohydrates: 2 g	Protein: 0.5 g

1. In a large bowl, mash the avocados with a fork.
2. Mix in the rest of the ingredients until well blended. Taste and adjust seasonings as necessary.
3. Serve immediately, or store in the refrigerator until ready to use.

Sun-Dried Tomato Dip

This dip is wonderful to take to parties, and can easily be made the night before. Serve with pita chips or sliced vegetables.

 SERVES 16

Ingredients

½ cup chopped sun-dried tomatoes
¾ cup nonfat plain Greek yogurt
¼ cup reduced-fat mayonnaise
⅛ teaspoon garlic powder
½ teaspoon salt
¾ teaspoon ground black pepper
¼ cup torn fresh basil

Place all the ingredients except basil in a food processor or blender, and blend until fairly smooth. Add basil and blend for another minute. Refrigerate for at least 1 hour so flavors blend before serving.

PER SERVING

Calories: 17	Sugar: 1.75 g
Fat: 0.3 g	Fiber: 0.25 g
Cholesterol: 0.5 mg	Sodium: 147 mg
Carbohydrates: 2 g	Protein: 1 g

Spicy Black Bean Cilantro Dip

Even picky eaters will want to dive into this healthy bean dip. This can be served as an appetizer or healthy snack. You can adjust the seasonings and spices to suit your tastes.

 SERVES 15

Ingredients

1 (15-ounce) can black beans, drained

½ cup nonfat plain Greek yogurt

¼ cup tomato paste

½ cup salsa

½ teaspoon cumin

1½ teaspoons chopped cilantro

¼ teaspoon cayenne pepper

¼ cup crumbled feta cheese

Additional cilantro and chopped tomatoes, for garnish

PER SERVING

Calories: 55

Fat: 0.7 g

Cholesterol: 2.6 mg

Carbohydrates: 8.5 g

Sugar: 1 g

Fiber: 1.5 g

Sodium: 103 mg

Protein: 3.6 g

1. Mash beans in a medium bowl until chunky. Add Greek yogurt, tomato paste, salsa, cumin, cilantro, and cayenne pepper. Mix well. Cover and refrigerate for at least 30 minutes.
2. Sprinkle with feta cheese just before serving. Garnish with cilantro and chopped tomatoes if desired.

GREEK VEGETABLE PIZZA

This appetizer is so simple, yet so tasty. You can easily add cooked, diced chicken if you'd like, or experiment with your favorite vegetables and cheeses. Chopped mint is an excellent garnish, and melds well with the Greek flavors of this dish.

 SERVES 8

Ingredients

4 (6") flour tortillas
Olive oil, as needed
1 recipe Tzatziki Dip (see recipe in this chapter)
½ cup seeded and chopped plum tomatoes
½ cup chopped avocado
⅓ cup chopped black olives
⅓ cup chopped green onions
¾ cup crumbled feta cheese

PER SERVING

Calories: 161	Sugar: 2.25 g
Fat: 10.6 g	Fiber: 1 g
Cholesterol: 14 mg	Sodium: 417 mg
Carbohydrates: 11.25 g	Protein: 6 g

1. Preheat the grill to medium-high heat. Brush one side of each tortilla with olive oil, and place the oiled side down on the heated grill. Grill tortillas for 2 minutes, and brush the tops with oil. Turn the tortillas over, and spread 2–3 tablespoons tzatziki over each tortilla. Layer the remaining toppings over the tzatziki.

2. Close the grill and cook for 2–3 minutes until the cheese has melted. Remove the pizzas from the grill, let cool for 3–5 minutes, and slice into quarters to serve.

Green Onions and Scallions

Which is the correct term: green onions or scallions? These are actually the same vegetable with two different names. They have a mildly sweet onion flavor and are a wonderful addition to many dishes. Green onions contain fiber, vitamin A, vitamin C, and potassium.

Chunky Tomato Soup with Fresh Basil

Tomato soup lovers won't miss the cream in this soup! Greek yogurt is a much healthier substitute for cream, and enhances the smooth, tangy taste you're looking for in tomato soup.

SERVES 4

Ingredients

1 tablespoon butter

1 small yellow onion, diced

2 cloves garlic, minced

2 (14.5-ounce) cans fire-roasted diced tomatoes

1 cup chicken broth

1 cup low-fat milk

1 cup nonfat plain Greek yogurt

1 teaspoon sugar

½ teaspoon ground black pepper

3 teaspoons minced fresh basil

1½ teaspoons fresh thyme leaves

Grated Parmesan cheese for topping, if desired

1. In a large saucepan, melt the butter. Sauté the onion and garlic for 5–8 minutes over medium heat until the onions are translucent.
2. Add the rest of the ingredients except Parmesan cheese, stirring frequently so everything is thoroughly mixed.
3. Simmer on low for 30 minutes. Serve immediately. Top with grated Parmesan cheese if desired.

PER SERVING

Calories: 156

Fat: 5.25 g

Cholesterol: 15.5 mg

Carbohydrates: 16 g

Sugar: 7 g

Fiber: 2.25 g

Sodium: 479 mg

Protein: 12.25 g

Gluten-Free Crab Cakes

These are perfect served as an entrée over a bed of greens, or you can easily make them smaller and serve them as an appetizer. They're great paired with lemon wedges and Tabasco sauce, or even served as sandwiches on gluten-free rolls.

YIELDS 8 SMALL CRAB CAKES

Ingredients

1 tablespoon plus ½ cup extra-virgin olive oil

2 green onions, finely chopped

12 ounces jumbo lump crabmeat (do not use imitation; it is not gluten-free)

2 cloves garlic, chopped

2 eggs

1 tablespoon reduced-fat, gluten-free mayonnaise

1½ cups gluten-free bread crumbs, divided use

½ teaspoon ground cayenne pepper

½ teaspoon ground basil

½ teaspoon ground oregano

Salt and freshly ground black pepper, to taste

1. Heat 1 tablespoon oil in a medium skillet over medium-high heat. Sauté green onions for 1–2 minutes, until tender. Remove from heat.
2. In a large bowl, combine the crabmeat, garlic, eggs, mayonnaise, ½ cup bread crumbs, cayenne pepper, basil, oregano, salt, and pepper. Form into 8 small patties, about ½" thick.
3. In a separate bowl, place 1 cup of bread crumbs. Dredge patties in the bread crumbs thoroughly.
4. Heat ½ cup oil in a skillet over medium-high heat. Place the crab cakes in oil and cook until golden brown, about 3–4 minutes, making sure to cook evenly on both sides. Once cooked, place on paper towels to drain. Serve with Garlic Aioli Sauce (see recipe in this chapter). (Ensure that all ingredients used for sauce are also gluten-free.)

PER SERVING WITH GARLIC AIOLI SAUCE

Calories: 331	Sugar: 6 g
Fat: 21 g	Fiber: 1 g
Cholesterol: 95 mg	Sodium: 730 mg
Carbohydrates: 23 g	Protein: 14 g

Garlic Aioli Sauce

This sauce is perfect for dipping, and works well as a delicious spread on sandwiches.

 SERVES 6

Ingredients

½ cup reduced-fat mayonnaise

2 tablespoons nonfat plain Greek yogurt

3 cloves garlic, chopped

2 tablespoons freshly squeezed lemon juice

½ teaspoon salt

½ teaspoon ground pepper

¼ teaspoon dried cumin

Place all the ingredients in a small bowl and mix until thoroughly blended. Refrigerate for at least 1 hour so the flavors blend completely.

PER SERVING

Calories: 41

Fat: 1.3 g

Cholesterol: 0 mg

Carbohydrates: 6.6 g

Sugar: 4 g

Fiber: 0 g

Sodium: 383 mg

Protein: 0.6 g

CREAMY VEGETABLE QUINOA SOUP

This wonderful vegetarian soup will impress even the most serious carnivores. Feel free to use whatever vegetables you have in the house.

Ⓥ SERVES 6

Ingredients

2 tablespoons butter
½ cup chopped onion
2 cloves garlic, minced
½ cup diced carrot
½ cup diced celery
¼ cup diced zucchini
1 (15.5-ounce) can crushed tomatoes
4 cups low-sodium vegetable broth
1 tablespoon dried parsley
1 teaspoon dried thyme
1 tablespoon dried basil
½ cup quinoa, rinsed and drained
1 cup low-fat milk
½ cup nonfat plain Greek yogurt
3 tablespoons flour
¼ cup grated Parmesan cheese, for topping

1. In a large saucepan, melt the butter. Add the onion and garlic, and cook over medium heat for 2–3 minutes until they soften. Add the carrot, celery, zucchini, tomatoes, and broth. Stir to combine.
2. Add parsley, thyme, and basil, and bring to a boil. Mix thoroughly, and lower the heat to a simmer. Add the quinoa.
3. In a small bowl, add the milk, Greek yogurt, and flour; stir until smooth. Pour the milk mixture into pan and cover. Mix well so everything is combined.
4. Simmer on low for 25–30 minutes until the quinoa is tender. Garnish with Parmesan cheese if desired.

PER SERVING

Calories: 190	Sugar: 3 g
Fat: 7 g	Fiber: 5 g
Cholesterol: 18 mg	Sodium: 510 mg
Carbohydrates: 22 g	Protein: 10.5 g

ZUCCHINI STICKS

These zucchini sticks are baked, not fried, and still have a crispy texture. These are delicious enough for entertaining, and no one will suspect that they are healthy!

 SERVES 6

Ingredients

2 large zucchini

2 eggs

¼ cup nonfat plain Greek yogurt

¼ teaspoon garlic powder

¼ teaspoon onion powder

⅛ teaspoon salt

⅛ teaspoon ground black pepper

¼ teaspoon oregano

1½ cups panko bread crumbs

PER SERVING, NOT INCLUDING DIP

Calories: 161	Sugar: 2 g
Fat: 2.6 g	Fiber: 2 g
Cholesterol: 71 mg	Sodium: 166 mg
Carbohydrates: 27 g	Protein: 7.5 g

1. Preheat the oven to 400°F. Prepare 2 large baking sheets with parchment paper.
2. Slice a zucchini in half lengthwise. Slice each half again lengthwise, and then again lengthwise. You should have 8 long sticks total. Cut each of them in half, for 16 sticks total. Repeat with the second zucchini.
3. In a medium shallow bowl, combine the eggs and Greek yogurt and mix well until smooth.
4. In another medium shallow bowl, mix the garlic powder, onion powder, salt, pepper, and oregano. Mix well. Add bread crumbs and mix again.
5. Take a zucchini stick and coat it in the egg mixture. Then roll it in the bread crumb mixture, and place onto a baking sheet. Repeat until all the zucchini sticks are covered.
6. Bake for 25 minutes, until golden brown, carefully turning over halfway through the baking time. Serve immediately with Creamy Ranch Dip (see recipe in this chapter).

CREAMY RANCH DIP

This dip is perfect for dipping sliced vegetables, crackers, or even spicy buffalo chicken wings. Unlike other ranch dips made with mayonnaise or buttermilk, this one is high in protein and low in fat.

 YIELDS 1 CUP

Ingredients

1 teaspoon ground parsley
½ teaspoon onion powder
½ teaspoon garlic powder
⅛ teaspoon salt
⅛ teaspoon ground black pepper
⅛ teaspoon dried thyme
1 teaspoon minced onion
¼ teaspoon dried dill weed
¼ teaspoon dried chives
1 cup nonfat plain Greek yogurt

In a small bowl, mix all the seasonings together. Add the Greek yogurt and mix well. Refrigerate for 30 minutes and serve cold.

PER TABLESPOON

Calories: 9	Sugar: 0.5 g
Fat: 0 g	Fiber: 0 g
Cholesterol: 0 mg	Sodium: 23 mg
Carbohydrates: 0.7 g	Protein: 1.5 g

Onion Dill Dip

You won't feel guilty reaching for a second serving of this dip. Traditional onion dips are loaded with saturated fats and unhealthy ingredients, but this version is low in fat and full of flavor.

YIELDS 1 CUP

Ingredients

1 teaspoon ground parsley

½ teaspoon onion powder

½ teaspoon garlic powder

⅛ teaspoon salt

⅛ teaspoon ground black pepper

1 teaspoon minced onion

¼ teaspoon dried dill weed

¼ teaspoon dried chives

¾ cup nonfat plain Greek yogurt

¼ cup reduced-fat sour cream

¼ teaspoon Worcestershire sauce

In a small bowl, mix all the seasonings together. Add Greek yogurt, sour cream, and Worcestershire sauce and mix well. Refrigerate for at least 30 minutes or overnight, and serve cold.

PER TABLESPOON

Calories: 12

Fat: 0.44 g

Cholesterol: 2 mg

Carbohydrates: 0.7 g

Sugar: 0.38 g

Fiber: 0 g

Sodium: 25 mg

Protein: 1.25 g

CHEESY EGGPLANT ROUNDS

This wonderful appetizer is not only simple to prepare, but it's also very tasty. This recipe complements a Greek menu nicely, but is impressive enough to serve as a stand-alone appetizer at your next cocktail party.

 SERVES 6

Ingredients

1 large eggplant, sliced into rounds, approximately 1" thick

2 tablespoons grapeseed oil

¼ teaspoon salt

⅛ teaspoon ground black pepper

½ cup crumbled feta cheese

½ cup nonfat plain Greek yogurt

3 cloves garlic, minced

2 tomatoes, chopped

Fresh dill weed, for topping

PER SERVING

Calories: 116	Sugar: 4 g
Fat: 7.5 g	Fiber: 3.6 g
Cholesterol: 12 mg	Sodium: 247 mg
Carbohydrates: 8.5 g	Protein: 5 g

1. Preheat the oven to 350°F. Spray a large casserole dish with organic nonstick cooking spray.
2. Season the eggplant rounds with the oil, salt, and pepper, and place them in the casserole dish.
3. Bake the eggplant for 10 minutes, so it is soft but still sturdy.
4. In a small bowl, mix the feta cheese, Greek yogurt, and garlic.
5. Arrange the eggplant rounds on a platter. Spread the Greek yogurt mixture on top of each round. Add a teaspoon of chopped tomatoes on top of the yogurt mixture. Top with fresh dill weed. Serve immediately, or refrigerate until ready to serve. This recipe can be served warm or cold.

ROASTED VEGETABLE TART

This light appetizer is perfect for summer nights. You can experiment with different cheeses if you'd like—try adding shredded pepper jack for a spicy kick, or crumbled feta for a creamier result.

 YIELDS 12 TARTS

Ingredients

2 plum tomatoes, sliced

1 zucchini, sliced

1 cup sliced mushrooms

1 cup cubed butternut squash

1 clove garlic, minced

¼ teaspoon salt

¼ teaspoon ground black pepper

2 tablespoons olive oil, divided use

8 sheets phyllo pastry

¼ cup nonfat plain Greek yogurt

½ cup shredded mozzarella

½ cup shredded Cheddar cheese

1 tablespoon grated Parmesan cheese

2 tablespoons chopped fresh basil

PER TART

Calories: 107

Fat: 6 g

Cholesterol: 8 mg

Carbohydrates: 9.6 g

Sugar: 1.2 g

Fiber: 0.8 g

Sodium: 175 mg

Protein: 4.6 g

1. Preheat the oven to 400°F.
2. Place vegetables, garlic, salt, and pepper on a large baking sheet. Mix well. Drizzle 1 tablespoon olive oil over the top of the vegetables and mix again. Roast for 20–25 minutes until tender. Allow to cool.
3. Grease a 9" × 13" casserole dish and lay 6 sheets of phyllo pastry inside. Sparingly brush with the remaining olive oil. Spread the Greek yogurt on top of the phyllo dough evenly. Sprinkle the shredded mozzarella, then the Cheddar, over the yogurt.
4. Pour the cooled vegetables on top of the cheese and spread evenly.
5. Crumble the remaining 2 phyllo sheets on top of the vegetable mixture. Sprinkle the Parmesan cheese and basil on top.
6. Bake for 15 minutes until the edges are golden brown. Allow to cool, and slice into 12 squares. Serve warm or cold.

BUTTERNUT SQUASH APPLE SOUP

This slightly sweet, creamy soup is perfect any time of the year, and delivers amazing health benefits. Butternut squash is high in dietary fiber and is loaded with vitamin C and vitamin A, which are powerful antioxidants that help keep your immune system strong. Ginger is commonly used to treat stomach discomfort, and also has anti-inflammatory properties.

 SERVES 6

Ingredients

2 tablespoons virgin coconut oil

4 cloves garlic, minced

1 large onion, minced

2 large butternut squash, peeled, seeded, and cubed

2 tablespoons minced fresh gingerroot

3 cups reduced-sodium vegetable broth

2 cups water

3 apples, cored, peeled, and chopped

1½ teaspoons salt

½ teaspoon ground black pepper

Plain Greek yogurt and diced green onions, for garnish

PER SERVING, WITHOUT GARNISH

Calories: 167	Sugar: 4.2 g
Fat: 5.5 g	Fiber: 5 g
Cholesterol: 0 mg	Sodium: 865 mg
Carbohydrates: 31 g	Protein: 3.7 g

1. In a large stockpot, add the coconut oil. Cook the garlic and onion for 3–4 minutes over medium heat until they soften. Add the squash, and cook for 5 minutes until the squash browns a bit.

2. Add ginger, vegetable broth, water, apples, salt, and pepper, and bring to a boil. Lower the heat, and simmer for 30 minutes uncovered until the squash softens.

3. Working in batches, place the butternut squash mixture in a blender or food processor and blend until smooth. Or, use an immersion blender to blend the ingredients. Be very careful while working with the hot soup! Add water if needed. To serve, garnish each dish with a dollop of Greek yogurt and diced green onions. Add more salt and pepper if desired.

Healthy Fats

Many people are afraid of cooking with fats, even ones that are healthy for them. Studies show that coconut oil can help keep cholesterol levels low, it may prevent certain diseases, and may even help with weight loss. Other plant-based oils contain high cholesterol and trans fats, but coconut oil does not. Look for "virgin coconut oil" on the label. This means that fresh coconut was used without any chemical processing.

Chapter 4

SMOOTHIES

There is nothing more refreshing than a delicious, ice-cold smoothie. Smoothies are increasingly popular these days; besides being quick, easy, and convenient to take with you, they are also incredibly healthy and nutritious. Smoothies can be enjoyed any time of the year and can supplement any meal, whether it's breakfast, lunch, or dinner. Greek yogurt adds a great deal of protein to help create a perfectly well-balanced snack, and with its creamy texture, it makes a velvety, smooth drink. Smoothies are also a great way to give your picky little ones the necessary vitamins and minerals found in fruits and vegetables. That's right, vegetables. In this chapter, we explore the many different varieties of smoothies that combine vegetables, fruits, seeds, and nut butters. Smoothies are an easy way to get creative in the kitchen and a fun way to let your children be your taste testers. All you need is a simple blender and you're ready to start experimenting.

Green Tea Smoothie

Who says you can't use green tea for smoothies too? Now you can get all the health benefits of green tea in a delicious smoothie.

 SERVES 2

Ingredients

2 green tea bags

1½ cups hot water

1 frozen banana

½ cup frozen pineapple (unsweetened)

1 teaspoon honey

½ avocado, peeled and pitted

½ cup nonfat vanilla Greek yogurt

2 cups torn kale

1 cup ice

PER SERVING

Calories: 262

Fat: 8.5 g

Cholesterol: 0 mg

Carbohydrates: 41.5 g

Sugar: 14 g

Fiber: 7 g

Sodium: 106 mg

Protein: 10 g

1. Steep tea bags in hot water for at least 3 minutes; let cool. Discard the tea bags, and place the tea in the blender.
2. Add the remaining ingredients to the blender in the order shown. Blend until smooth. Serve immediately.

Drink Green Tea for Better Health

Green tea is loaded with antioxidants, and studies suggest that green tea might prevent certain cancers and even heart disease. Studies show that green tea helps fight obesity by lowering LDL ("bad") cholesterol and lowering blood pressure.

Kiwi Pineapple Smoothie

This is a great way to sneak leafy green vegetables into your smoothies. You can't even taste the spinach!

 SERVES 2

Ingredients

1 cup frozen pineapple (unsweetened)

2 kiwis, peeled and chopped

½ frozen banana

¾ cup nonfat plain Greek yogurt

½ cup pineapple juice

½ cup ice (use less if using frozen fruits)

1 cup torn spinach

1 tablespoon ground flaxseed

Place all ingredients in the blender as listed in the order shown. Blend until smooth. Serve immediately.

PER SERVING

Calories: 232	Sugar: 22.5 g
Fat: 2 g	Fiber: 5 g
Cholesterol: 4 mg	Sodium: 46.5 mg
Carbohydrates: 45 g	Protein: 11.5 g

FLAX BERRY SMOOTHIE

This smoothie is naturally sweet from the raspberries and banana. It's a perfect healthy breakfast for those hectic mornings when you don't have a lot of time to cook.

 SERVES 2

Ingredients

1 cup nonfat vanilla Greek yogurt

½ cup frozen raspberries

½ cup fat-free milk

½ frozen banana

2 tablespoons ground flaxseed

Place all ingredients in the blender as listed in the order shown. Blend until smooth. Serve immediately.

PER SERVING

Calories: 192

Fat: 3 g

Cholesterol: 1 mg

Carbohydrates: 27 g

Sugar: 15.5 g

Fiber: 4.5 g

Sodium: 84 mg

Protein: 15 g

Chocolate Peanut Butter Smoothie

Don't even tell the kids how healthy this smoothie is—it tastes like a dessert in a glass! The creamy combination of natural peanut butter, almond milk, and Greek yogurt will give your kids the protein their bodies need to grow and play.

 SERVES 2

Ingredients

2 tablespoons unsweetened cocoa powder

2 tablespoons natural peanut butter

½ frozen banana

½ cup almond milk

½ cup nonfat vanilla Greek yogurt

½ cup ice

PER SERVING

Calories: 208	Sugar: 10 g
Fat: 10 g	Fiber: 3.5 g
Cholesterol: 0 mg	Sodium: 116 mg
Carbohydrates: 22.5 g	Protein: 10.5 g

Combine all ingredients in the blender as listed in the order shown. Blend until thick and creamy. Serve immediately.

VERY BERRY HEMP SMOOTHIE

This simple smoothie is delicious and satisfying. You can substitute another frozen fruit for the berries if you'd like.

 SERVES 2

Ingredients

1 cup frozen mixed berries, unsweetened

1 tablespoon ground hemp seeds

¾ cup nonfat vanilla Greek yogurt

½ cup almond milk

1 teaspoon honey

PER SERVING

Calories: 152	Sugar: 15.5 g
Fat: 2 g	Fiber: 2.5 g
Cholesterol: 0 mg	Sodium: 77 mg
Carbohydrates: 23 g	Protein: 10 g

Combine all ingredients in the blender as listed in the order shown. Blend until smooth. Serve immediately.

All about Hemp Seeds

What are hemp seeds? These little seeds are found in hemp plants, and are not just edible but also extremely healthy. They contain all the essential amino acids your body needs, which makes them a perfect protein source for vegans. In addition, they are packed with essential fatty acids, antioxidants, and fiber. You can buy hemp seeds in health food stores and some specialty grocery stores.

Piña Colada Smoothie

This tropical drink is a perfect beginning to an ordinary day. The protein in the quinoa and Greek yogurt will help keep you full until lunch time, and the chia seeds contain omega-3 fatty acids, antioxidants, and fiber.

 SERVES 2

Ingredients
¾ cup nonfat plain Greek yogurt
½ cup chopped frozen mango
1½ cups frozen pineapple chunks
1 tablespoon quinoa flakes
1 tablespoon chia seeds
1 tablespoon shredded coconut
½ cup almond milk

PER SERVING

Calories: 227	Sugar: 32 g
Fat: 3 g	Fiber: 4.5 g
Cholesterol: 4 mg	Sodium: 71 mg
Carbohydrates: 40 g	Protein: 11.5 g

Place all ingredients in the blender as listed in the order shown. Blend until smooth. Serve immediately.

REFRESHING GRAPEFRUIT SMOOTHIE

This fruity smoothie is packed with antioxidants (vitamin C) and protein. It's perfect for breakfast or as a mid-morning snack.

 SERVES 2

Ingredients

1 ruby red grapefruit, sliced

1 ripe banana

¾ cup nonfat strawberry-banana Greek yogurt

1 tablespoon honey

1 cup ice

½ cup orange juice

2 tablespoons ground flaxseed

Place all ingredients in the blender as listed in the order shown. Blend until smooth. Serve immediately.

PER SERVING

Calories: 255	Sugar: 9.5 g
Fat: 3 g	Fiber: 3 g
Cholesterol: 0 mg	Sodium: 42 mg
Carbohydrates: 50 g	Protein: 9.5 g

Apple Pie Smoothie

This smoothie is sweet and tastes like you are drinking apple pie. Pink Lady and Granny Smith apples are tart and balance the sweet flavors, so they work best in this smoothie.

 SERVES 2

Ingredients

1 organic apple, chopped
½ cup nonfat vanilla or apple Greek yogurt
¼ cup almond milk
¼ cup apple juice
½ teaspoon ground cinnamon
1 tablespoon chia seeds

PER SERVING

Calories: 136
Fat: 1.5 g
Cholesterol: 0 mg
Carbohydrates: 24.5 g

Sugar: 7.5 g
Fiber: 4 g
Sodium: 47 mg
Protein: 6.5 g

Place all ingredients in the blender as listed in the order shown. Blend until smooth. Serve immediately.

Use Your Apple Peels

Don't peel your apple before blending! The most amount of vitamins and fiber are found directly under the peel. But if you keep the peel on, you should seriously consider buying organic apples. Pesticides linger on the outer peels of apples that are not grown organically. Apples are on the Environmental Working Group's "Dirty Dozen" list for the top 12 fruits and vegetables that contain the most chemicals and pesticides. Therefore, it is best to buy organic.

Mint Chocolate Smoothie

This is a delicious recipe from my dear friend Robin, who blogs at *www.kneadtocook.com*. Robin is so talented and creative with her recipes, and this smoothie is just as creative—and delicious!

 SERVES 2

Ingredients

2 ripe bananas

1 scoop vegetarian vanilla protein powder

1 cup nonfat vanilla Greek yogurt

1 cup low-fat mint chocolate chip ice cream

8 ice cubes

1½ cups vanilla almond milk

1 tablespoon chia seeds

2 tablespoons chopped fresh mint leaves

1 tablespoon dark chocolate chips

PER SERVING

Calories: 478

Fat: 6.5 g

Cholesterol: 37 mg

Carbohydrates: 78 g

Sugar: 24 g

Fiber: 4 g

Sodium: 265 mg

Protein: 28.5 g

Place all ingredients in the blender except the chocolate chips and blend until the desired consistency is reached. Sprinkle with chocolate chips. Serve immediately.

Chia Power

Chia seeds have seen a tremendous growth in popularity recently for all of their health benefits. They are loaded with fiber, omega-3 fatty acids, protein, and antioxidants. They are simple to add to smoothies, and also offer wonderful texture to oatmeal and yogurt.

Green with Envy Smoothie

This is a great way to sneak greens into your picky kids. You can barely taste the spinach, and this counts as a full serving of vegetables!

SERVES 2

Ingredients

1½ cups chopped fresh baby spinach

1 cup chopped carrot

2 apples, cored, peeled, and chopped

1 ripe banana, preferably frozen

¼ cup fat-free milk

¾ cup nonfat plain Greek yogurt

1 teaspoon honey

1 tablespoon chia seeds

PER SERVING

Calories: 255

Fat: 2 g

Cholesterol: 0 mg

Carbohydrates: 53 g

Sugar: 27 g

Fiber: 6 g

Sodium: 116 mg

Protein: 11 g

Place all the ingredients in the blender as listed in the order shown. Blend until smooth. Serve immediately.

Storing Smoothies

Do you have some smoothie left over? You can place it in the refrigerator and drink it later, or simply freeze it for the next morning. You can freeze smoothies in individual cups with lids or in an airtight container. Just make sure you leave a little room in the container or cup because the smoothie may expand when freezing. Allow 6–8 hours for thawing.

Pumpkin Vanilla Smoothie

Food blogger and friend Robin, of *www.kneadtocook.com*, has created another incredible smoothie recipe, this time with a fun twist on pumpkin and vanilla. With such incredible flavors—and pumpkin ice cream—how could you go wrong?

 SERVES 2

Ingredients
1 cup ice cubes
2 cups pumpkin ice cream
1½ cups vanilla almond milk
½ cup nonfat vanilla Greek yogurt
1 scoop vegetarian vanilla protein powder
½ teaspoon pumpkin spice

Place all ingredients in the blender as listed in the order shown. Blend until smooth. Serve immediately.

PER SERVING

Calories: 434	Sugar: 18 g
Fat: 14 g	Fiber: 2 g
Cholesterol: 71 mg	Sodium: 247 mg
Carbohydrates: 57 g	Protein: 23 g

POMEGRANATE BERRY SMOOTHIE

This smoothie is the perfect way to start your day. The combination of pomegranate and berries give just the right amount of sweetness.

 SERVES 2

Ingredients
½ cup pomegranate seeds
½ cup frozen mixed berries, unsweetened
¾ cup nonfat honey Greek yogurt
½ cup almond milk
½ cup ice

PER SERVING

Calories: 142	Sugar: 23 g
Fat: 0.5 g	Fiber: 1 g
Cholesterol: 0 mg	Sodium: 76 mg
Carbohydrates: 26 g	Protein: 7.5 g

Place all ingredients in the blender as listed in the order shown. Blend until smooth. Serve immediately.

Choose Pomegranates for Immune Health
Pomegranates are filled with fiber and vitamin C. Since they're packed with vitamin C, they're a wonderful immune system booster. You can easily buy the seeds themselves in grocery stores, or take the seeds out yourself. Simply cut a whole pomegranate in half, and spoon the seeds out of both halves.

Peanut Butter Banana Smoothie

Kids and adults will love this smoothie—what's not to like with peanut butter and bananas? It's delicious, but also loaded with healthy fat, protein, and potassium.

 SERVES 2

Ingredients

2 tablespoons natural peanut butter

1 frozen banana

¾ cup nonfat vanilla Greek yogurt

¼ cup fat-free milk

2 tablespoons ground flaxseed

PER SERVING

Calories: 268

Fat: 10.5 g

Cholesterol: 0 mg

Carbohydrates: 28.5 g

Sugar: 10.5 g

Fiber: 4 g

Sodium: 108 mg

Protein: 14.5 g

Combine all the ingredients in the blender as listed in the order shown. Blend until smooth. Serve immediately.

Choosing Natural Peanut Butter

All peanut butters are not the same. Even the ones labeled "natural" might have added sugars and oils in them. Read your ingredient labels: It should only say peanuts (and salt, if desired). If the label says there is no need to stir, it means the peanut butter is not 100 percent natural.

Coconut Almond Smoothie

The natural sweetness of coconut and the nuttiness of the almonds make the perfect flavor combination. This may remind you of a certain classic candy bar, but this smoothie is much healthier!

 SERVES 2

Ingredients

1 tablespoon shredded coconut

1 tablespoon sliced almonds

2 tablespoons natural almond butter

¾ cup nonfat vanilla Greek yogurt

1 tablespoon chia seeds

½ cup almond milk

PER SERVING

Calories: 247	Sugar: 13 g
Fat: 14 g	Fiber: 3 g
Cholesterol: 0 mg	Sodium: 79 mg
Carbohydrates: 18.5 g	Protein: 12.5 g

Place all ingredients in the blender as listed in the order shown. Blend until smooth. Serve immediately.

OATMEAL COOKIE DOUGH SMOOTHIE

Love cookie dough but don't like all the extra fat and calories? This is an easy and healthy way to satisfy your sweet tooth! This smoothie contains all-natural ingredients, including almond butter. Almond butter is loaded with vitamin E, magnesium, iron, and protein. Drink up!

 SERVES 2

Ingredients

¾ cup nonfat vanilla Greek yogurt

½ banana

½ teaspoon ground cinnamon

½ teaspoon pure vanilla extract

½ cup oats

½ cup fat-free milk

1 tablespoon natural almond butter

2 tablespoons semi-sweet chocolate chips, divided use

1 cup ice

Combine Greek yogurt, banana, cinnamon, vanilla, oats, milk, almond butter, 1 tablespoon chocolate chips, and ice in the blender. Blend until smooth. Divide into 2 glasses, and top smoothies with remaining chocolate chips. Serve immediately.

PER SERVING

Calories: 251

Fat: 8.5 g

Cholesterol: 2 mg

Carbohydrates: 35.3 g

Sugar: 19 g

Fiber: 2.5 g

Sodium: 71 mg

Protein: 14.3 g

Carrot Ginger Apple Smoothie

The pretty orange color of this smoothie makes a stunning presentation. The natural sweetness of carrots blends perfectly with the apple, and the gingerroot adds a bit of spice.

V **SERVES 2**

Ingredients

1 cup chopped or shredded carrots

1 apple, cored and chopped

¾ cup nonfat vanilla Greek yogurt

¼ cup apple juice

½" fresh gingerroot, chopped or grated

1 cup ice

PER SERVING

Calories: 147

Fat: 0.5 g

Cholesterol: 0 mg

Carbohydrates: 27.5 g

Sugar: 18 g

Fiber: 3 g

Sodium: 85 mg

Protein: 9 g

Combine all the ingredients in the blender as listed in the order shown. Blend until smooth. Serve immediately.

The Healing Powers of Ginger

Gingerroot may not be the nicest-looking spice, but it has substantial benefits. Most commonly known for helping calm nausea, ginger is filled with antioxidants and minerals such as potassium and magnesium. In addition to its health benefits, ginger makes a tasty complement to both sweet and savory recipes.

BLUEBERRY PEAR SMOOTHIE

This delightful smoothie is not only an exotic purple color, but it's also loaded with vitamins, minerals, and protein.

 SERVES 2

Ingredients

1 cup frozen blueberries, unsweetened

1 pear, chopped

¾ cup nonfat pear or vanilla Greek yogurt

1 tablespoon chia seeds

¼ cup fat-free milk

½ cup ice

Place all ingredients in the blender as listed in the order shown. Blend until smooth. Serve immediately.

PER SERVING

Calories: 186	Sugar: 25 g
Fat: 1.5 g	Fiber: 6 g
Cholesterol: 0 mg	Sodium: 55 mg
Carbohydrates: 33.5 g	Protein: 10.5 g

Chapter 5

ENTRÉES

Your main course is arguably the most important part of your meal, and serving balanced, healthful entrées at home is more important than ever in the age of supersized portions and fat-laden dishes. In this chapter, you will see how Greek yogurt can add wonderful flavor and texture to a variety of entrées in a healthy way. Greek yogurt makes a delightful substitution for sour cream, milk, or cream in many of your favorite recipes. Add Greek yogurt to your hamburgers and you will be amazed at how juicy and flavorful they are. Are you hesitant to eat chicken pot pie because of all of the fat? Worried about the calories in cream sauces and creamed soups? Greek yogurt adds the perfect blend of texture, flavor, and nutrition while eliminating the unnecessary fat and calories found in typical rich dishes. You will be amazed how easily Greek yogurt can be substituted in your favorite hearty meals without sacrificing the flavors you love. The recipes in this chapter are sure to please even the pickiest eaters!

Indian-Style Lentils with Chicken

This wonderfully blended dish is packed with protein, and will keep you full for hours.

SERVES 6

Ingredients

1 cup lentils

3 cups water

½ teaspoon salt, divided use

1 teaspoon pepper

2 cloves garlic, peeled and minced

1 medium onion, peeled and finely minced

2 tablespoons lemon juice

1 teaspoon cumin

¼ teaspoon red pepper flakes

½ cup chopped fresh parsley

1 pound boneless, skinless chicken breasts, cut into bite-size pieces

1 cup low-fat plain Greek yogurt

1 tablespoon curry powder

1 teaspoon Tabasco sauce

1. Preheat the broiler. Line a baking sheet with aluminum foil.
2. Place the lentils and water in a medium saucepan. Bring to a boil, reduce heat, and simmer.
3. Just before the lentils are cooked (when barely tender, after about 25 minutes), add ¼ teaspoon salt, pepper, garlic, onion, lemon juice, cumin, red pepper flakes, and parsley.
4. In a medium bowl, toss the chicken with the Greek yogurt, curry powder, remaining salt, and Tabasco sauce. Place the chicken on the foil-lined baking sheet and broil for 5 minutes per side.
5. Mix the chicken into the lentils, and serve with rice or quinoa.

PER SERVING

Calories: 168	Sugar: 3 g
Fat: 2 g	Fiber: 3.5 g
Cholesterol: 45 mg	Sodium: 268 mg
Carbohydrates: 12 g	Protein: 25 g

ENCHILADA CASSEROLE

This flavorful casserole is perfect for entertaining. You can adjust the spices to suit your taste and your guests' preferences.

SERVES 6

Ingredients

2 tablespoons extra-virgin olive oil

½ medium onion, chopped

1 clove garlic, minced

2 pounds lean ground beef

1 tablespoon chili powder

1 tablespoon cumin

⅛ teaspoon ground cayenne pepper

1 tablespoon chopped fresh cilantro

1 (15-ounce) can black or pinto beans, thoroughly rinsed and drained

1 cup diced tomatoes or 1 (14-ounce) can diced tomatoes

½ cup diced green pepper

1 large carrot, shredded

1 (4-ounce) can diced green chili peppers

1 cup frozen corn

¼ teaspoon salt

8–12 corn tortillas (amount depends on how many you want to use)

2 cups reduced-fat shredded sharp Cheddar or Monterey Jack cheese

2 scallions, finely chopped

1 avocado, peeled, pitted, and sliced

1 cup nonfat plain Greek yogurt

½ cup sliced black olives

1 cup salsa

1. Preheat the oven to 425°F.
2. Heat the oil in a very large, deep skillet or Dutch oven, and cook the onion and garlic for 3–4 minutes until they soften.
3. Add the ground beef, chili powder, cumin, cayenne pepper, and cilantro, and cook for 5–8 minutes, until the beef turns brown.
4. Add the beans, tomatoes, green pepper, carrot, chili peppers, and corn. Season with salt and cook an additional 1–2 minutes until thoroughly combined.
5. Spray a 9" × 13" casserole dish with organic nonstick cooking spray. Layer half of the corn tortillas, half of the meat mixture, and then half of the cheese. Repeat again until all the ingredients are used.
6. Bake for 15 minutes until the cheese is melted. Top with scallions, avocado, Greek yogurt, olives, and salsa in even layers.

PER SERVING

Calories: 597	Sugar: 8 g
Fat: 24 g	Fiber: 10 g
Cholesterol: 88 mg	Sodium: 1,019 mg
Carbohydrates: 48 g	Protein: 52 g

Zesty Slow-Cooker Pork Chops and Mushrooms

These tender pork chops are simple to prepare and taste delicious. Your kitchen will smell wonderful all day while they're cooking.

SERVES 6

Ingredients

1½ pounds boneless center-cut pork chops (approximately 6 chops)

½ teaspoon salt

½ teaspoon ground black pepper

1 teaspoon garlic powder

¼ teaspoon ground paprika

½ cup all-purpose flour

2 tablespoons olive oil

1 yellow onion, chopped

1 (14.5-ounce) can low-sodium chicken broth

¼ cup vermouth

8 ounces sliced mushrooms

1 cup nonfat plain Greek yogurt

PER SERVING

Calories: 349

Fat: 12 g

Cholesterol: 95 mg

Carbohydrates: 14 g

Sugar: 2 g

Fiber: 0.8 g

Sodium: 302 mg

Protein: 41 g

1. Season the pork chops with salt, pepper, garlic powder, and paprika. Dredge the pork chops in the flour. Add the olive oil to a large skillet over medium-high heat. Place the chops in the pan.

2. Brown both sides of the chops for about 3–4 minutes each side and transfer to the slow cooker. Place the chopped onion on top of chops, and pour the chicken broth over the top.

3. Cook on high for 6 hours. When the pork chops are cooked, place them on a plate.

4. Pour the chicken broth mixture into a large skillet. Add vermouth and mushrooms, and cook over medium heat for a few minutes, stirring frequently. Remove from heat and add Greek yogurt. Stir well. Pour the sauce over the pork chops. Serve immediately.

Vermouth Substitutions

Don't have any vermouth in the house? No problem. You can use whatever dry white wine you have on hand. Sauvignon Blanc would be the best choice to cook with in this dish. It doesn't need to be an expensive wine—just one that is light and aromatic.

Savory Greek Burgers

You will love the healthy twist on these delicious, tangy burgers. Substituting oats for breadcrumbs adds flavor as well as fiber and nutrients.

YIELDS 6 BURGERS

Ingredients

1 pound lean, organic ground beef
½ cup nonfat plain Greek yogurt
¼ cup oats
1 tablespoon plus 1 teaspoon dried minced onions
2 beef bouillon cubes
½ teaspoon onion powder
½ teaspoon garlic powder
⅛ teaspoon salt
⅛ teaspoon ground black pepper
¼ teaspoon parsley flakes
⅛ teaspoon ground paprika

PER SERVING

Calories: 135	Sugar: 0.8 g
Fat: 4 g	Fiber: 0.8 g
Cholesterol: 40 mg	Sodium: 291 mg
Carbohydrates: 6 g	Protein: 18 g

1. In a large bowl, mix ground beef, Greek yogurt, and oats.
2. In a small bowl, mix all seasonings together, making sure to break up the beef bouillon cubes. Add the seasoning mixture to the beef combination and mix thoroughly with your hands. Cover and refrigerate while the grill heats up.
3. Preheat the grill to medium heat. Form the beef mixture into 6 balls, then flatten with your hand to form patties.
4. Grill 6–8 minutes on each side until cooked throughout (160°F), or until the meat reaches your desired doneness. Serve on whole-wheat rolls or soft pita, with lots of chopped tomatoes, lettuce, and olives on the side.

Choosing Quality Beef

All beef is not the same. Look for lean beef, not "hamburger beef." Hamburger beef is allowed added fats, but the fat found in ground beef occurs naturally. Choose extra-lean, organic, grass-fed beef for a healthier option. Also look for beef that has no added hormones or antibiotics, preferably USDA organic.

BEEF STROGANOFF

This wonderful classic dish can be served with noodles, rice, or quinoa. Feel free to use chopped turkey or chicken to reduce the fat content.

SERVES 6

Ingredients

2 tablespoons extra-virgin olive oil

1 medium onion, chopped

8 ounces button mushrooms, stems removed, brushed clean

2 cloves garlic, minced

2 tablespoons whole-wheat flour, plus ¼ cup for coating the meat

1 teaspoon dried mustard

Salt and pepper, to taste

1½ cups beef broth, warmed

1 cup dry red wine

1 teaspoon Worcestershire sauce

2 pounds filet mignon, cut into bite-size cubes

2 tablespoons unsalted butter

2 tablespoons snipped fresh dill weed

1 cup nonfat plain Greek yogurt

1. In a large sauté pan, heat the oil over medium heat. Add the onion, mushrooms, and garlic. Cook for 5 minutes to soften.
2. Add 2 tablespoons flour, mustard, salt, and pepper to the pan; stir to blend.
3. Mix in the warmed beef broth, and stir to thicken. Stir in the wine and Worcestershire sauce and bring to a boil. Turn off the heat.
4. On a large piece of waxed paper, roll the beef in ¼ cup flour.
5. Heat the unsalted butter in a separate sauté pan. Sear the beef in the butter for 1 minute to quickly brown and seal in the juices.
6. Spoon the beef into the mushroom sauce, add the dill weed, and stir to blend. Simmer for 10–15 minutes; the beef should be medium-rare.
7. Just before serving, stir in the Greek yogurt. Spoon over a bed of rice, noodles, or quinoa.

PER SERVING

Calories: 424	Sugar: 2 g
Fat: 17 g	Fiber: 1.3 g
Cholesterol: 108 mg	Sodium: 313 mg
Carbohydrates: 10 g	Protein: 49 g

Chicken Pot Pie

Using premade pie crusts and frozen vegetables for this chicken pot pie saves a lot of time—and the results are just as delicious. Just be cautious when choosing your prepared pie crusts; ultimately there should only be butter, flour, water, and a little salt. Many of them contain added preservatives, artificial colors and flavors, and hydrogenated fats. Look for a crust labeled "organic" with ingredients you can pronounce.

SERVES 8

Ingredients

1 box prepared pie crusts (set of 2 (10") pie crusts)

1 tablespoon butter

½ cup chopped onion

1 pound chicken breast, cooked and cubed

1 (10-ounce) bag frozen mixed vegetables

¼ teaspoon dried thyme

½ teaspoon salt

¼ teaspoon ground black pepper

1 (14.5-ounce) can low-sodium chicken broth

¼ cup nonfat plain Greek yogurt

1 cup fat-free milk

2 tablespoons flour

PER SERVING

Calories: 291	Sugar: 6.25 g
Fat: 13 g	Fiber: 2 g
Cholesterol: 37 mg	Sodium: 444 mg
Carbohydrates: 24 g	Protein: 18.5 g

1. Preheat the oven to 425°F. Take pie crusts out of the freezer and set aside.
2. Place the butter and onion in a large skillet, and cook for 2–3 minutes until the onions soften. Add the chicken and stir for 1–2 minutes until the mixture starts to brown. Add the vegetables, thyme, salt, and pepper. Stir and cook for 3–4 minutes.
3. Add the chicken broth and stir. Cook for another 5 minutes.
4. In a small bowl, add the Greek yogurt, milk, and flour. Mix well until smooth. Add this to the chicken broth mixture, stirring frequently. Cook another 5 minutes to thicken.
5. Prepare bottom part of the pie by spreading 1 crust onto a 9" pie plate. Fold the crust over the rim to allow complete coverage. Pour the chicken mixture into prepared pie crust.
6. Place other pie crust on top of mixture. Make sure the mixture is completely covered. Pinch the 2 crusts together around the edges. Cut a small slit on the top to allow steam to escape.
7. Bake for 30–35 minutes until the crust is golden brown and bubbly. Let cool 5 minutes before slicing.

Chicken Shortcuts

If you want to save even more time, use a rotisserie chicken! You can either shred or chop the chicken, and simply add it to the skillet to brown with the onion.

Skillet Taco Quinoa

This zesty, healthy, and hearty dish will add Mexican flair to your dinner table. You can adjust the seasonings to your taste. If you'd like it spicier, try adding some diced jalapeño pepper.

SERVES 4

Ingredients

2 tablespoons olive oil

¼ cup chopped onion

1 pound lean ground chicken

1 tablespoon chili powder

¼ teaspoon onion powder

¼ teaspoon garlic powder

⅛ teaspoon crushed red pepper

1 teaspoon ground cumin

1 teaspoon salt

1 teaspoon ground black pepper

½ cup water

1 (15.5-ounce) can black beans, rinsed and drained

½ cup frozen corn

2 plum tomatoes, seeded and diced

1 cup cooked quinoa

¼ cup chopped fresh cilantro

⅓ cup nonfat plain Greek yogurt

¼ cup reduced-fat shredded Cheddar cheese, for topping

1. Place the olive oil and onion in a large skillet. Sauté for 5–8 minutes over medium heat until the onions are translucent.
2. Add the ground chicken and cook for 6–8 minutes, breaking it into chunks, until no longer pink. Add seasonings, salt, pepper, and water, and stir to combine. Continue to cook for a few minutes until some of the water has been absorbed.
3. Add the black beans, corn, and tomatoes and mix well. Lower the heat; add the quinoa and cilantro, and then mix again. Simmer on low for 3–5 minutes. Remove from the heat and add the Greek yogurt. Mix well. Top with the cheese if desired, and serve immediately.

PER SERVING, WITH CHEDDAR CHEESE

Calories: 489	Sugar: 3 g
Fat: 12 g	Fiber: 8 g
Cholesterol: 96 mg	Sodium: 765 mg
Carbohydrates: 45.5 g	Protein: 46.5 g

Chicken in Cilantro Lime Cream Sauce

The cilantro lime cream sauce adds a great deal of flavor to the chicken in this dish. You won't believe that this isn't loaded with fat and calories like typical cream sauces—it tastes rich and indulgent, but is much healthier than its cream-based counterparts. Serve with brown rice or whole-wheat noodles.

YIELDS 6 CHICKEN BREASTS; SERVES 6

Ingredients

Chicken

3 tablespoons olive oil

6 chicken breasts, boneless and skinless (about 5 ounces each)

¼ teaspoon salt

¼ teaspoon ground black pepper

Sauce

1 cup low-sodium chicken broth

⅛ teaspoon salt

¼ teaspoon ground black pepper

2 cloves garlic, minced

1 teaspoon Dijon mustard

2 tablespoons torn fresh cilantro

1 cup nonfat plain Greek yogurt, room temperature

1. To prepare the chicken: Place the olive oil in a large nonstick skillet. Season the chicken breasts with salt and pepper and place in the skillet. Brown them for 5–7 minutes on each side until completely cooked through. Place on a plate and set aside.
2. To prepare the sauce: In a small bowl, combine the broth, salt, pepper, garlic, Dijon mustard, and cilantro; stir until smooth.
3. Pour half the Dijon mixture into the same skillet while continuing to stir. Place the cooked chicken in the skillet. Pour the remaining Dijon mixture on top of the chicken, making sure all the chicken is covered. Simmer on low for 15 minutes. Remove from the heat and add the Greek yogurt. Mix thoroughly. Serve immediately, and pour the extra sauce on top.

PER SERVING

Calories: 226	Sugar: 1 g
Fat: 7 g	Fiber: 0 g
Cholesterol: 82 mg	Sodium: 229 mg
Carbohydrates: 2 g	Protein: 37 g

Fiesta Meatloaf

This is a fun twist on your typical meatloaf. Using extra lean ground beef helps decrease the saturated fat, and the ground flaxseed adds fiber and omega-3 essential fatty acids.

SERVES 6

Ingredients

1½ pounds extra lean, organic ground beef

½ cup nonfat plain Greek yogurt

1 clove garlic, minced

½ cup finely chopped onion

¼ cup bread crumbs

¼ cup ground flaxseed (optional)

1 tablespoon chili powder

1½ teaspoons cumin

1 teaspoon oregano

¼ teaspoon red pepper flakes

½ teaspoon onion powder

¼ teaspoon salt

½ teaspoon black pepper

½ teaspoon paprika

1. Preheat the oven to 375°F and grease a 9" × 5" loaf pan with organic nonstick cooking spray.
2. In a large bowl, mix the ground beef, Greek yogurt, garlic, onion, bread crumbs, and flaxseed.
3. In a small bowl, mix seasonings together. Add the seasoning mixture to beef combination, and mix thoroughly with your hands.
4. Place the meat into the prepared loaf pan and cook for 45 minutes until no longer pink inside. Let rest for 5 minutes before slicing.

Meatloaf Safety Tips

Are you still not sure that your meatloaf is fully cooked? Place an instant-read thermometer in the middle of the loaf. To avoid contamination from eating undercooked meat, the temperature should be at least 160°F.

PER SERVING, WITHOUT FLAXSEED

Calories: 185	Sugar: 2 g
Fat: 6 g	Fiber: 1.2 g
Cholesterol: 60 mg	Sodium: 246 mg
Carbohydrates: 7 g	Protein: 25 g

Lemon Yogurt and Basil Chicken Kebabs

This recipe is a wonderful creation from my friend Carrie, an incredible food blogger at *www .carriesexperimentalkitchen.blogspot.com*. The fresh flavors blend perfectly together to create this healthy dish.

SERVES 4

Ingredients

¾ cup nonfat lemon Greek yogurt

1½ tablespoons chopped fresh basil

Zest and juice of 1 lemon

1 teaspoon kosher salt

¼ teaspoon ground black pepper

10 boneless chicken tenders, cut into thirds

10–12 skewers

10 ounces mushrooms, wiped clean and cut in half

1 red onion, cut into 2" pieces

1 medium zucchini, cut in half lengthwise then sliced into ½" slices

4 plum tomatoes, cut in half lengthwise then sliced into 1" slices

1. In a medium bowl, combine the Greek yogurt, basil, lemon zest and juice, salt, and pepper and mix well.
2. Place the chicken in a large resealable plastic bag and add the yogurt mixture; coat the chicken well and refrigerate for at least 2 hours.
3. If you are using wooden skewers, soak them in water for 30 minutes prior to grilling so the wood doesn't burn when cooking on the grill.
4. Layer the mushrooms, onion, zucchini, tomatoes, and chicken on the skewers. Discard the remaining marinade.
5. Grill the kebabs for 15–20 minutes, or until the chicken is cooked through.

PER SERVING

Calories: 162	Sugar: 8 g
Fat: 1 g	Fiber: 2 g
Cholesterol: 50 mg	Sodium: 488 mg
Carbohydrates: 11.75 g	Protein: 28 g

ALMOND CRUSTED CHICKEN

There's no need to fry this crispy baked chicken. The sliced almonds add a wonderful, crunchy texture. Almond flour (also known as almond meal) is a light, gluten-free flour that can be found in specialty stores and most grocery stores.

SERVES 6

Ingredients

½ cup nonfat plain Greek yogurt

2 eggs

¼ teaspoon garlic powder

¼ teaspoon onion powder

⅛ teaspoon salt

¼ teaspoon ground black pepper

½ teaspoon dried oregano

½ cup bread crumbs

¼ cup ground flaxseed

½ cup almond flour

1 tablespoon grated Parmesan cheese

2 tablespoons sliced or slivered almonds

6 chicken breasts, boneless and skinless (about 5 ounces each)

1. Preheat the oven to 350°F. Grease a 9" × 13" casserole dish.
2. In a shallow medium bowl, mix the Greek yogurt and eggs until smooth. In another shallow medium bowl, combine the remaining ingredients except the chicken.
3. Dip each chicken breast in the Greek yogurt mixture, and then in bread crumb mixture, and lay in the casserole dish. Sprinkle any remaining bread crumb mixture on top of the chicken.
4. Bake for 30–35 minutes until chicken centers are no longer pink and the juices run clear. Serve immediately.

PER SERVING

Calories: 334	Sugar: 2 g
Fat: 13 g	Fiber: 3 g
Cholesterol: 152 mg	Sodium: 282 mg
Carbohydrates: 12 g	Protein: 42 g

Tilapia in Garlic Butter Sauce

This dish is so simple to prepare and yet so delicious. With only 6 ingredients, it's easy enough to make on a busy night during the week.

SERVES 4

Ingredients

2 tablespoons butter

1 small onion, diced

2 cloves garlic, minced

½ cup nonfat plain Greek yogurt

1 tablespoon fresh lemon juice

1 pound tilapia filets

Fresh parsley, for garnish

PER SERVING

Calories: 224	Sugar: 2 g
Fat: 9 g	Fiber: 0 g
Cholesterol: 81 mg	Sodium: 116 mg
Carbohydrates: 3.5 g	Protein: 33 g

1. Preheat the oven to 350°F.
2. Cook the butter, onion, and garlic in a small skillet for 3–4 minutes over medium heat until translucent.
3. Place half of the butter mixture in the bottom of a 9" × 13" casserole dish and spread it around evenly.
4. Pour the other half of the butter mixture into a small bowl. Stir in the Greek yogurt and lemon juice and mix well.
5. Place the tilapia filets in the casserole dish on top of the butter mixture.
6. With a large spoon or spatula, spread the Greek yogurt mixture on top of the filets. Bake for 30 minutes until the edges are brown and the fish flakes with a fork. Garnish with fresh parsley if desired. Serve immediately.

GRILLED SIRLOIN WITH CREAMY HORSERADISH SAUCE

This steak has lots of flavor, especially when marinated overnight. The creamy horseradish sauce serves as the perfect dip with just enough seasonings.

SERVES 8

Ingredients

Marinade
2 cloves garlic, minced

2 tablespoons Worcestershire sauce

2 tablespoons fresh lemon juice (about 1 lemon)

1 tablespoon nonfat plain Greek yogurt

½ teaspoon ground black pepper

1 tablespoon Dijon mustard

Meat
2 pounds boneless sirloin filets with fat trimmed off

Dipping Sauce
¼ cup nonfat plain Greek yogurt

¼ cup sour cream

4 tablespoons prepared horseradish

1 teaspoon Dijon mustard

2 tablespoons diced fresh chives

1. In a small bowl, mix all the ingredients for the marinade. Stir well. Place the filets in a large resealable bag, and pour the marinade mixture on top. Shake and move around so all the meat is coated. Place in the refrigerator and marinate for several hours or overnight.
2. Place all the ingredients for dipping sauce in a small bowl and mix well. Cover and refrigerate until ready to eat.
3. Prepare the grill, and place the filets on the grill over medium heat. Discard the remaining marinade. Grill the filets for 20–25 minutes, or until desired doneness is reached, turning over once. Cover with aluminum foil and let stand 15 minutes before eating. Serve with the creamy horseradish sauce.

PER SERVING, WITH SAUCE

Calories: 216	Sugar: 1.6 g
Fat: 7 g	Fiber: 0 g
Cholesterol: 55 mg	Sodium: 156 mg
Carbohydrates: 2 g	Protein: 34 g

TASTY BABY RACK OF LAMB

Don't be intimidated by this fantastic entrée. You can marinate the lamb for several hours or overnight and it will still taste divine.

SERVES 4

Ingredients

2 teaspoons dried parsley
½ teaspoon onion powder
½ teaspoon garlic powder
½ teaspoon dried oregano
½ cup low-fat plain Greek yogurt
2 tablespoons Dijon mustard
2 (8-bone-in) racks of lamb
2 tablespoons extra-virgin olive oil
1 teaspoon salt
½ teaspoon ground black pepper
1 teaspoon chopped fresh mint
Fresh mint and low-fat Greek yogurt, for topping

PER SERVING

Calories: 251	Sugar: 1.5 g
Fat: 14 g	Fiber: 0 g
Cholesterol: 91 mg	Sodium: 715 mg
Carbohydrates: 2.5 g	Protein: 26 g

1. Preheat the oven to 425°F.
2. In a medium bowl, mix the dried parsley, onion powder, garlic powder, dried oregano, ½ cup Greek yogurt, and mustard until well combined. Place the lamb in a medium-size airtight container, and spread the Greek yogurt mixture all over the top and bottom. Close the container and place in the refrigerator for at least 2 hours. Take the lamb out of the refrigerator and let sit at room temperature for 30 minutes before cooking.
3. Heat the oil in a large skillet over medium heat for 1 minute. Place the lamb in the skillet fat side down, and sear for 3–5 minutes until browned. If the skillet isn't large enough to fit both racks of lamb, cook them one at a time. Turn the rack over, and cook the other side for 2 minutes. When both sides are seared, place in a large baking dish.
4. In a small bowl, mix together the salt, pepper, and 1 teaspoon mint. Sprinkle this mixture all over both sides of the lamb. Place the baking dish in the preheated oven for 12–18 minutes, until the meat reaches an internal temperature of 125–130°F.
5. Remove the lamb from the oven, and let sit at room temperature for 20 minutes, loosely covered with aluminum foil. To serve, slice into individual chops and top with a dollop of Greek yogurt and chopped fresh mint, if desired.

CHEESY RICE AND BEANS

The beans and Greek yogurt provide enough protein to make this simple, well-balanced dish a complete meal. When rice and beans are combined, they create a complete protein, which means they contain all the essential amino acids. Amino acids are the building blocks of protein, and protein is essential for muscle building and tissue repair.

 SERVES 8

Ingredients

2 cups cooked brown rice

1 (15-ounce) can black beans, drained and rinsed

1 (15-ounce) can pinto beans, drained and rinsed

1 cup corn

2 plum tomatoes, diced

¼ cup minced green onion

1 green bell pepper, diced

1 cup shredded Mexican cheese blend, divided use

1 teaspoon oregano

1 teaspoon cumin

½ teaspoon chili powder

Juice of ½ lime

¼ cup chopped fresh cilantro, divided use

½ cup nonfat plain Greek yogurt

¼ cup sour cream

Sliced avocado, for garnish

1. Preheat the oven to 350°F. Grease a 2-quart casserole dish and set aside.

2. In a large bowl, mix together the rice, beans, corn, tomatoes, onion, pepper, ½ cup cheese, oregano, cumin, chili powder, lime juice, 2 tablespoons cilantro, Greek yogurt, and sour cream. Mix well so all ingredients are combined. Pour into the prepared casserole dish.

3. Top with the remaining cheese and cilantro and bake for 30 minutes until golden brown. Garnish with fresh avocado slices, if desired.

PER SERVING

Calories: 272	Sugar: 3 g
Fat: 7 g	Fiber: 9 g
Cholesterol: 16 mg	Sodium: 117 mg
Carbohydrates: 40 g	Protein: 15 g

Mushroom Squash Stew

This light vegetarian dish is very versatile; you can add beans to boost the protein, or serve it over brown rice. Meat lovers can add sliced sausage for a complete meal.

 SERVES 6

Ingredients
2 tablespoons olive oil

1 small onion, chopped

3 cloves garlic, minced

2 red bell peppers, chopped

3 cups cleaned, sliced baby bella mushrooms

3 cups cubed butternut squash

1 teaspoon dried oregano

½ teaspoon salt

½ teaspoon ground black pepper

¼ cup sour cream

¼ cup nonfat plain Greek yogurt

1. Place the olive oil, onion, and garlic in a large skillet. Cook for 3–4 minutes until softened.
2. Add the red peppers, mushrooms, squash, oregano, salt, and pepper. Mix well; cook for 10 minutes until vegetables soften, while continuing to stir.
3. Once the vegetables are tender, remove from the heat. Add the sour cream and Greek yogurt and mix thoroughly. Serve immediately.

Mushroom Prep

How do you clean mushrooms? Mushrooms are like sponges, so do not soak them in water—they will get soggy. Simply take a wet paper towel and wipe them clean.

PER SERVING

Calories: 157	Sugar: 6 g
Fat: 7 g	Fiber: 6.5 g
Cholesterol: 0 mg	Sodium: 225 mg
Carbohydrates: 19 g	Protein: 6.5 g

Mexican Casserole

This dish can be served as a vegetarian entrée or as a side dish next to enchiladas, tacos, or burritos. The flavors blend together so nicely, and you can adjust the seasonings to suit your taste.

 SERVES 6

Ingredients

¾ cup uncooked rice

1 (14.5-ounce) can vegetable broth

1¼ cups sour cream

¼ cup nonfat plain Greek yogurt

1 teaspoon chili powder

1 teaspoon ground cumin

¼ teaspoon onion powder

¼ teaspoon garlic powder

⅛ teaspoon dried oregano

⅛ teaspoon crushed red pepper flakes

½ teaspoon salt

½ teaspoon ground black pepper

¾ cup shredded Cheddar cheese, divided use

1 cup corn

1 (15-ounce) can black beans, drained and rinsed

1 (15-ounce) can pinto beans, drained and rinsed

1 cup diced plum tomatoes

2 (4-ounce) cans diced green chili peppers, drained

¼ cup torn and chopped fresh cilantro

PER SERVING

Calories: 492	Sugar: 2.5 g
Fat: 17 g	Fiber: 10 g
Cholesterol: 37 mg	Sodium: 863 mg
Carbohydrates: 63 g	Protein: 23 g

1. Preheat the oven to 350°F. Prepare a 9" × 13" casserole dish with organic nonstick cooking spray.
2. In a large pot or Dutch oven, bring the rice and vegetable broth to a boil. Reduce the heat to low, cover, and simmer for 15 minutes until almost all broth is absorbed into the rice. The rice should be al dente.
3. In a medium bowl, combine the sour cream, Greek yogurt, and seasonings. Add salt and pepper, and stir until well combined.
4. Add the sour cream mixture to the pot with the rice. Add ½ cup cheese, corn, beans, tomatoes, chili peppers, and cilantro. Mix well.
5. Pour the mixture into the prepared casserole dish and top with the remaining cheese.
6. Bake uncovered for 25–30 minutes until the cheese is bubbly. Let cool for 5 minutes before serving.

Broccoli Cheese Rice Bake

This wonderful vegetarian casserole can easily be made with diced cooked chicken to please the meat lovers. It can be prepared hours before you'd like to serve it; just place it in the refrigerator until you are ready to bake.

 SERVES 6

Ingredients
2 pounds broccoli, about 3–4 heads, chopped

½ medium onion, chopped

1 cup uncooked brown rice

1 (14-ounce) can vegetable broth

1 cup nonfat plain Greek yogurt

½ teaspoon ground basil

3 cloves garlic, minced

1 cup shredded sharp Cheddar cheese, divided use

1 tablespoon bread crumbs

PER SERVING

Calories: 290	Sugar: 4 g
Fat: 8.5 g	Fiber: 6.5 g
Cholesterol: 22 mg	Sodium: 634 mg
Carbohydrates: 36 g	Protein: 19 g

1. Preheat the oven to 350°F. Grease a 1½-quart casserole dish.
2. Place ¼" water in a large skillet and bring to a boil. Add chopped broccoli and onion. Cover and cook for 3 minutes until the broccoli is bright green and crunchy. Set aside.
3. Place the rice and broth in a large pot and bring to a boil. Cover and lower the heat. Let simmer for 20 minutes or until the broth is absorbed. Remove from heat.
4. Add Greek yogurt, basil, garlic, and ¾ cup cheese to the rice. Mix well until thoroughly combined. Pour into the prepared casserole dish. Top with remaining ¼ cup cheese and bread crumbs. Bake for 20–25 minutes until golden brown. Serve immediately.

Garlic's Benefits
Is garlic really that good for you? The answer is yes! Studies may suggest that regular consumption of both raw and cooked garlic may help prevent certain cancers and help to lower cholesterol.

ROASTED TOMATO GALETTE

This lovely vegetarian galette is the perfect alternative to pizza. Store-bought pizza dough saves a lot of time and preparation work—look for whole-wheat varieties to maximize the nutrition of this dish.

 SERVES 6

Ingredients

1 (16-ounce) package whole-wheat pizza dough
1 pint red cherry tomatoes, halved
1 pint yellow cherry tomatoes, halved
¼ cup chopped onion
2 cloves garlic, minced
2 tablespoons chopped fresh basil
½ teaspoon salt
½ teaspoon ground black pepper
2 tablespoons olive oil
1 tablespoon balsamic vinegar
¾ cup nonfat plain Greek yogurt
¾ cup part-skim ricotta cheese
1 egg
1 tablespoon fat-free milk
1 tablespoon grated fresh Parmesan cheese

PER SERVING

Calories: 314	Sugar: 3 g
Fat: 11 g	Fiber: 5 g
Cholesterol: 47 mg	Sodium: 617 mg
Carbohydrates: 40 g	Protein: 14 g

1. Preheat the oven to 400°F. Grease a 9" × 13" casserole dish and round pizza stone.
2. Roll the pizza dough on the stone to create a large circle.
3. In a medium bowl, combine the tomatoes, onion, garlic, basil, salt, pepper, olive oil, and balsamic vinegar; mix well. Pour the tomato mixture into the prepared casserole dish. Bake for 15 minutes until softened.
4. In the same bowl, mix together the Greek yogurt and ricotta cheese. Spread the cheese mixture onto the pizza dough as you would spread sauce onto a pizza, leaving a 2" border around the edges.
5. When the tomatoes are done, place them in the middle of the dough on top of the cheese mixture. Fold the 2" edge over the filling, pleating as you go around.
6. In a small bowl, beat the egg and milk together well until completely blended. Brush the egg mixture lightly over the edges of the dough. Top with Parmesan cheese and bake for 30 minutes until the edges are golden brown. Let cool for 5 minutes before serving.

Egg Wash Essentials

Brushing the edges of the dough with the egg mixture helps to give a beautiful, shiny, golden color. You can also use 1 tablespoon of water in the egg wash if you don't have any milk. It's crucial to make sure that the egg is completely beaten when preparing an egg wash. If it isn't completely beaten, there will be chunks of eggs on your dough, which may alter the flavor of your galette.

Spinach Avocado Goat Cheese Quesadillas

This unique blend of flavors makes for a delicious appetizer or main dish. You can boost the nutrition of these quesadillas by adding chopped tomatoes, sweet corn, or bell peppers to the spinach mixture, or spoon in some black beans for added fiber and protein.

 SERVES 4

Ingredients

¼ cup goat cheese

¼ cup nonfat plain Greek yogurt

1 tablespoon olive oil

2 cloves garlic, minced

½ cup chopped green onion

4 cups baby spinach

2 avocados, seeded and sliced

4 (7") flour tortillas

PER SERVING

Calories: 365	Sugar: 5 g
Fat: 25 g	Fiber: 9.5 g
Cholesterol: 12 mg	Sodium: 216 mg
Carbohydrates: 29 g	Protein: 11 g

1. In a small bowl, mix together the goat cheese and Greek yogurt. Set aside.
2. In a large skillet, add the oil. Sauté the garlic and onion for 3–4 minutes over medium heat until soft. Add spinach and cook 2–3 minutes until wilted. Place spinach mixture in a bowl and set aside, leaving as much oil in the pan as possible. Lower heat.
3. On half of each tortilla, spread the cheese mixture. Then layer with sliced avocado and the spinach mixture. Fold tortillas over and place in the skillet. Cook on medium-low heat for 5 minutes on each side until golden brown. Serve immediately.

Chapter 6

SIDE DISHES

You found your perfect entrée, but what should you serve with it? The side dish is just as important as the entrée for creating nutritionally balanced, wholesome meals. From Mashed Sweet Potatoes to Zucchini Kale Fritters, this chapter has a variety of delicious recipes to help you choose the right side dish to complement your meal. Greek yogurt takes the guesswork out by enhancing the flavor and boosting the nutrition of your typical side dishes. If you are hesitant about enjoying coleslaw at your holiday meals, don't be! By simply replacing the cream and butter with Greek yogurt, you'll maintain the creaminess of the dish while eliminating all that extra fat. Do you love sour cream on your potatoes? Try Greek yogurt instead—it has the same texture as sour cream, but without all the extra fat and calories. This chapter provides wonderful and healthy side dish recipes that will accompany any entrée, enhanced with the scrumptious flavor and incredible nutrition of Greek yogurt!

CREAMY COLESLAW

This is an updated version of classic coleslaw. You won't miss the fat and calories found in typical mayonnaise-based coleslaws.

 SERVES 12

Ingredients

1 pound shredded white cabbage

½ cup shredded carrots

1¾ cups nonfat plain Greek yogurt

½ cup apple cider vinegar

¼ cup turbinado sugar

1 tablespoon Dijon mustard

3 tablespoons dried minced onion

PER SERVING

Calories: 55	Sugar: 3.6 g
Fat: 0 g	Fiber: 1 g
Cholesterol: 0 mg	Sodium: 60.7 mg
Carbohydrates: 10 g	Protein: 4.1 g

1. In a large bowl, combine the cabbage and carrots.
2. In a medium bowl, combine the remaining ingredients. Pour the Greek yogurt mixture over the cabbage and carrots. Mix well and chill for 30 minutes before serving.

Choosing Apple Cider Vinegar

Don't just use any type of apple cider vinegar. Look for one that is raw and organic. Studies show that apple cider vinegar can help support the immune system, help rid your body of toxins, and possibly even help with weight loss.

Mashed Sweet Potatoes

Sweet potatoes are packed with vitamin C, calcium, beta-carotene, and potassium. They're a healthier choice than white potatoes because they have a lower glycemic index, which means they have less of a spiking effect on blood sugar levels when you eat.

V SERVES 6

Ingredients

2½ pounds sweet potatoes, scrubbed clean, unpeeled and quartered

2 tablespoons butter, softened

4 tablespoons nonfat plain Greek yogurt

1½ tablespoons fat-free milk

2 tablespoons sour cream

1 teaspoon salt

½ teaspoon ground cinnamon

2 tablespoons 100 percent pure maple syrup

Chopped green onion, for garnish

1. Place the potatoes in a large saucepan. Cover with water and bring to a boil over high heat. Once boiling, cover and reduce heat to low. Simmer for 20–25 minutes, until the potatoes are fork-tender.

2. Drain the potatoes thoroughly and place back into the saucepan.

3. In a small bowl, add the butter, Greek yogurt, milk, sour cream, salt, cinnamon, and maple syrup. Stir to combine.

4. Pour the Greek yogurt sauce over the potatoes and mix well. Mash with a potato masher or hand mixer on medium-high speed until desired consistency. Top with chopped green onions. Serve immediately.

PER SERVING

Calories: 251	Sugar: 22 g
Fat: 5 g	Fiber: 7 g
Cholesterol: 13 mg	Sodium: 498 mg
Carbohydrates: 47 g	Protein: 5.5 g

CREAMED SPINACH

Now there is no reason to feel guilty about eating this side dish. Greek yogurt makes a wonderful substitution for cream in this recipe.

Ⓥ SERVES 10

Ingredients

3 (10-ounce) bags fresh spinach, chopped

¼ cup butter

3 cloves garlic, minced

1 medium shallot, minced

½ cup nonfat plain Greek yogurt

½ cup grated Asiago cheese

½ cup grated Parmesan cheese

Salt and pepper, to taste

PER SERVING

Calories: 117	Sugar: 0.8 g
Fat: 8 g	Fiber: 2 g
Cholesterol: 23 mg	Sodium: 259 mg
Carbohydrates: 5 g	Protein: 7 g

1. Place the spinach in a large stockpot, cover with water, and cook over medium-high heat until wilted, about 2–3 minutes. Remove from heat and drain in a colander until most of the liquid is gone.
2. Place the butter in a large skillet and melt over medium heat. Add the garlic and shallot, and cook 3–4 minutes, until the shallot is translucent.
3. Add the spinach and slowly pour in the Greek yogurt. Sprinkle in the Asiago and Parmesan cheeses. Continue to stir until the sauce thickens, about 4–5 minutes. Season with salt and pepper. Serve warm or hot.

All about Shallots

Shallots have a wonderful flavor that tastes like a combination of garlic and onion. They resemble garlic with cloves, and are packed with vitamin C, vitamin B, and manganese. Choose shallots that are firm with dry exteriors, and avoid ones that are soft or ones with sprouts.

SPICY CORN BREAD STUFFED WITH CHEESE

This is a wonderful variation on typical corn bread. You can adjust the spices according to your taste. Try serving it with your next batch of veggie chili, or alongside a roasted chicken.

Ⓥ SERVES 8

Ingredients

1 cup cornmeal (yellow or white)

1 cup all-purpose flour

¼ cup light brown sugar

3 teaspoons baking powder

1 teaspoon salt

¼ teaspoon cumin

1 teaspoon dried red pepper flakes, or to taste

½ cup low-fat buttermilk

½ cup nonfat plain Greek yogurt

2 eggs, beaten

2 tablespoons melted unsalted butter

½ cup grated pepper jack or Cheddar cheese

PER SERVING

Calories: 233	Sugar: 8 g
Fat: 8 g	Fiber: 1.6 g
Cholesterol: 69 mg	Sodium: 590 mg
Carbohydrates: 33 g	Protein: 8.25 g

1. Preheat the oven to 400°F. In a large bowl, mix together the cornmeal, flour, sugar, baking powder, salt, cumin, and red pepper flakes.
2. Mix in the buttermilk, Greek yogurt, eggs, and melted butter.
3. Prepare an 8" square baking pan with organic nonstick cooking spray. Place half of the batter in the pan. Sprinkle with cheese. Cover with the rest of the batter. Bake for 20–25 minutes.

CREAMY ASIAGO POLENTA

Polenta is a great alternative to your ordinary side dishes, and can break you out of a typical potatoes-and-rice rut. Try using other cheeses, such as Cheddar or Parmesan, and adding chopped veggies for added flavor and nutrition.

 SERVES 4

Ingredients

1 cup cold water
½ cup corn grits or polenta
1 cup fat-free cold milk
½ teaspoon salt
2 tablespoons butter
¼ cup nonfat plain Greek yogurt
⅓ cup grated Asiago cheese
Fresh parsley, for garnish

1. In a small bowl, mix together the cold water and grits.
2. In a medium saucepan, bring the milk and salt to a boil. Slowly add the grits mixture while stirring continuously to prevent lumps. Cover and reduce heat to low. Simmer and cook 20 minutes, continuing to stir every few minutes to prevent sticking.
3. Remove from the heat, and stir in the butter, Greek yogurt, and cheese; mix well. Garnish with parsley, if desired. Serve immediately.

PER SERVING

Calories: 192	Sugar: 3.25 g
Fat: 9 g	Fiber: 0 g
Cholesterol: 27 mg	Sodium: 495 mg
Carbohydrates: 19 g	Protein: 8 g

Big Fat Greek Stuffed Sweet Potato

Food blogger Carrie, of *www.carriesexperimentalkitchen.blogspot.com*, has created another exciting and delicious recipe. Who says potatoes have to be stuffed with unhealthy ingredients? You'll love Carrie's twist on this!

 SERVES 4

Ingredients

2 large sweet potatoes

½ cup crumbled feta cheese, divided use

¼ cup nonfat plain Greek yogurt

1 tablespoon fresh parsley

¼ teaspoon salt

¼ teaspoon ground black pepper

PER SERVING

Calories: 141

Fat: 4.25 g

Cholesterol: 17 mg

Carbohydrates: 20 g

Sugar: 9 g

Fiber: 3.25 g

Sodium: 394 mg

Protein: 6 g

1. Scrub the potato skins under warm water, then pierce the skins in several places with a fork or the tip of a sharp knife to allow steam to escape. Place the potatoes on a microwave-safe dish lined with a napkin or paper towel. Microwave on high for 8–10 minutes, or until the insides are soft when pierced with a knife.

2. Remove the potatoes and cut in half lengthwise. Scoop out the flesh and place in a bowl. Place the skins in an oven-safe dish.

3. Add ¼ cup of the cheese, Greek yogurt, parsley, salt, and pepper to the potatoes and mash well. (The back of the fork works well; just whip until creamy.)

4. Place the potato mixture back into the shells, sprinkle with the remaining feta cheese, and broil for 2–3 minutes until the cheese has started to melt. Serve immediately.

Tomato Asparagus Bean Medley

This light and simple dish is perfect to serve at a cookout next to your favorite grilled meats. This can easily be made in advance and refrigerated until ready to serve.

 SERVES 6

Ingredients

1 pound asparagus, edges trimmed, and cut in half

1 (14-ounce) can cannellini beans, drained and rinsed

2 cloves garlic, minced

¼ cup minced red onion

1 tablespoon fresh lemon juice

½ teaspoon salt

¼ teaspoon ground black pepper

1 tablespoon chopped fresh basil

1 pint grape tomatoes, halved

3 tablespoons nonfat plain Greek yogurt

2 tablespoons sunflower seeds

1. Place the asparagus spears in a large skillet and cover with about 1" of water. Bring to a boil, reduce heat to low, and simmer for 3–4 minutes until crisp, tender, and bright green.
2. In a large bowl, mix together the beans, garlic, onion, lemon juice, salt, pepper, and basil. Add the asparagus and tomatoes and combine. Fold in the Greek yogurt and mix well. Sprinkle with sunflower seeds. Serve immediately, or refrigerate until ready to serve.

PER SERVING

Calories: 148	Sugar: 4 g
Fat: 3 g	Fiber: 7 g
Cholesterol: 0 mg	Sodium: 346 mg
Carbohydrates: 23 g	Protein: 9.5 g

Lemon Orzo with Toasted Pine Nuts

This side dish is packed with flavor and makes a beautiful presentation.

 SERVES 8

Ingredients

1 (16-ounce) box orzo

1 tablespoon grapeseed oil

Juice of ½ lemon

1 clove garlic, finely chopped

Salt and pepper, to taste

½ cup nonfat plain Greek yogurt

Zest of 2 lemons

1 tablespoon toasted pine nuts

¼ cup fresh parsley

1 tablespoon grated Parmesan cheese

PER SERVING

Calories: 203	Sugar: 2 g
Fat: 3.75 g	Fiber: 2 g
Cholesterol: 1.25 mg	Sodium: 17 mg
Carbohydrates: 33 g	Protein: 7.5 g

1. Cook the orzo in salted water according to package directions. Drain well. Do not run under water.
2. In a small bowl, mix the grapeseed oil and lemon juice.
3. Transfer the orzo to a serving bowl. Add the garlic, drizzle with the oil and lemon juice, and season with salt and pepper. Add the Greek yogurt and stir until combined.
4. Add lemon zest, pine nuts, and parsley, and toss. Top with Parmesan cheese if desired.

Zucchini Kale Fritters

These irresistible fritters are perfect next to any chicken or pork dish. Vegetarians can enjoy these alone over mixed greens as an entrée.

 YIELDS 25 SMALL FRITTERS

Ingredients

2 medium zucchini, peeled and shredded

4 cups trimmed and chopped kale

2 cloves garlic, minced

2 tablespoons diced green onion

2 eggs, lightly beaten

½ cup nonfat plain Greek yogurt

¼ cup seasoned bread crumbs

¼ cup ground flaxseed

¼ cup grated Parmesan cheese

½ teaspoon salt

¼ teaspoon ground black pepper

¼ cup extra-virgin olive oil

PER FRITTER

Calories: 53	Sugar: 0.44 g
Fat: 3.5 g	Fiber: 0.8 g
Cholesterol: 18 mg	Sodium: 115 mg
Carbohydrates: 3 g	Protein: 2 g

1. In a medium bowl, combine the zucchini, kale, garlic, onion, eggs, and Greek yogurt. In a small bowl, mix together the bread crumbs, flaxseed, Parmesan cheese, salt, and pepper. Slowly add the bread crumb mixture to the zucchini mixture.
2. Place 2–3 paper towels on a baking tray. Set aside.
3. In a large skillet, heat the oil over medium-high heat for 1 minute. Place small spoonfuls of the zucchini mixture into the hot skillet, spreading them down to make 3" fritters. Cook each side for 3 minutes until brown, making sure to turn over once. Drain the fritters on the prepared baking tray. Serve immediately.

Mexican Quinoa Stuffed Peppers

These make a perfect side dish or a vegetarian entrée. Quinoa is filled with protein and is also gluten-free, which makes it a wonderful option for vegetarians or those with a wheat allergy.

V SERVES 6

Ingredients

2 tablespoons extra-virgin olive oil

2 cloves garlic, minced

1 medium onion, minced

2 medium tomatoes, diced

1 (15-ounce) can black beans, drained and rinsed

¾ cup uncooked quinoa, rinsed and drained

2 cups water

1 tablespoon ground cumin

⅛ teaspoon red pepper flakes

¼ teaspoon chili powder

½ cup nonfat plain Greek yogurt

¼ cup torn and chopped cilantro

4 large red, yellow, or orange bell peppers, sliced in half lengthwise, seeds and ribs removed, stems intact

1 cup shredded Mexican blend cheese

Extra Greek yogurt and cilantro, for topping

1. Preheat the oven to 350°F.
2. Heat the oil in large skillet over medium heat for 1 minute. Add the garlic and onion and cook for 3–4 minutes until soft. Add tomatoes and continue to cook for another 3–4 minutes. Add the cumin, red pepper flakes, and chili powder and mix well.
3. Stir in the black beans, quinoa, and water. Bring to a boil, cover, and reduce heat. Simmer on low for 20 minutes until the liquid is absorbed. Remove from the heat. Slowly add the Greek yogurt and cilantro; stir to combine.
4. Stuff the peppers with the quinoa mixture, and place in a large baking dish. Cover loosely with aluminum foil and bake for 30 minutes. Remove the foil, sprinkle each pepper half with 1 tablespoon cheese, and bake for another 15 minutes. Let stand 5 minutes before serving. Top with a dollop of Greek yogurt and cilantro, if desired.

PER SERVING

Calories: 373	Sugar: 8 g
Fat: 13 g	Fiber: 8.5 g
Cholesterol: 21 mg	Sodium: 144 mg
Carbohydrates: 48 g	Protein: 17.5 g

CREAMY CORN CASSEROLE

This casserole is a perfect side dish for Thanksgiving dinner, and is much healthier than the traditional fat-laden varieties. Feel free to add diced onions and green pepper to the mixture for color and added flavor, or top with cooked crumbled bacon if you're feeling decadent. This recipe is great to make ahead of time; just refrigerate until you're ready to bake.

 SERVES 8

Ingredients

2 eggs

1 cup nonfat plain Greek yogurt

3 tablespoons butter, melted

¼ cup fat-free milk

¼ cup all-purpose flour

2 tablespoons turbinado sugar

½ teaspoon salt

⅛ teaspoon ground black pepper

2 cups corn

PER SERVING

Calories: 144	Sugar: 6 g
Fat: 6.6 g	Fiber: 1 g
Cholesterol: 66 mg	Sodium: 238 mg
Carbohydrates: 16 g	Protein: 6.5 g

1. Preheat the oven to 350°F. Grease a 9" × 9" casserole dish.
2. In a large bowl, mix all the ingredients except corn together until combined. Add the corn, and fold until just combined.
3. Bake for 55 minutes until the middle is set and the edges are golden brown. Let sit for 15 minutes before serving, and serve warm.

Chapter 7

SALADS

When you're eating healthy foods, many "salad" dishes seem like the best choices, whether you're eating at a cookout, dining at a restaurant, or cooking at home. But just as with appetizers, side dishes, and entrées, salads can have hidden fats and calories you may not be aware of. Many people will eat salad, believing that it is a healthier option, but creamy salads and dressings are typically high in saturated fat. Even low-fat salad dressings are loaded with unnecessary additives, sugars, fats, and sodium. By preparing your own salads and dressings with Greek yogurt, you will cut out all of these needless and incredibly unhealthy additions. If you stopped eating potato salad, tuna salad, and egg salad because you are trying to eat healthier, now you can enjoy these once-forbidden foods again—without the guilt. Greek yogurt is a perfect replacement for the mayonnaise in these dishes, without sacrificing the creamy texture and flavor. Armed with the recipes in this chapter, you'll want to bring the macaroni salad to your next barbecue, or Waldorf salad to your next picnic. You will be amazed at how easy it is to prepare these classic salads with a healthier twist! If you use Greek yogurt, you won't have to compromise flavor when trying to maintain your healthy lifestyle.

Avocado Egg Salad

There is no need for mayonnaise—and its added fat and calories—in this salad. The avocado not only adds to the creamy texture but also contains heart-healthy fats, vitamins, and minerals.

 SERVES 6

Ingredients

7 hard-boiled eggs, peeled and cooled

1 avocado, peeled, pitted, and cut into 1" pieces

2 tablespoons low-fat plain Greek yogurt

2 tablespoons lemon juice

1 green onion, finely chopped

1 celery stalk, finely chopped

1 teaspoon paprika

½ teaspoon salt

½ teaspoon pepper

PER SERVING

Calories: 159	Sugar: 2 g
Fat: 11.5 g	Fiber: 3 g
Cholesterol: 248 mg	Sodium: 275 mg
Carbohydrates: 6 g	Protein: 9 g

1. Separate the whites and the yolks of the eggs. Set aside 3 yolks for another use. Dice the egg whites.
2. In a large bowl, combine the avocado, egg yolks, and Greek yogurt. Mash until the mixture is creamy and smooth.
3. Mix in the lemon juice, onion, celery, paprika, salt, and pepper.
4. Gently add the chopped egg whites and fold to combine. Refrigerate or serve immediately.

CURRIED CHICKEN SALAD

Robin of *www.kneadtocook.com* shared this wonderful twist on a typical mayonnaise-loaded salad. The Greek yogurt adds a similar texture, without all the extra fat and calories. Thanks again, Robin!

SERVES 8

Ingredients

1½ pounds organic chicken tenders, cooked and shredded

3 teaspoons curry powder

1 tablespoon fresh lime juice

2 teaspoons honey

¼ cup chopped dried cherries

¼ teaspoon salt

¼ teaspoon ground black pepper

½ teaspoon ground cayenne pepper

¾ cup nonfat plain Greek yogurt

2 green onions, chopped

Add all the ingredients to a medium bowl and mix until well combined. Refrigerate in a covered container. Serve with crackers, bread, or pita bread.

PER SERVING

Calories: 88	Sugar: 4.5 g
Fat: 0.4 g	Fiber: 1.6 g
Cholesterol: 25 mg	Sodium: 190 mg
Carbohydrates: 7 g	Protein: 14 g

White Bean Salad Wrap

Move over creamy, fat-laden salads! This one is packed with protein and fiber.

 YIELDS 1 CUP SALAD

Ingredients

1 (15.5-ounce) can small white beans, drained and rinsed

1 clove garlic, chopped

½ cup chopped red onion

3 tablespoons nonfat plain Greek yogurt

1 tablespoon Dijon mustard

½ cup chopped carrots

2 tablespoons chopped fresh chives

Romaine lettuce, sliced tomatoes, and tortilla wraps, to serve

PER ½ CUP SALAD

Calories: 301	Sugar: 5 g
Fat: 0.5 g	Fiber: 12.5 g
Cholesterol: 1 mg	Sodium: 193 mg
Carbohydrates: 54 g	Protein: 20 g

1. Place beans in a small bowl and mash with a fork. Place beans, garlic, onion, Greek yogurt, Dijon mustard, carrots, and chives in blender or food processor. Blend until chunky, but not completely smooth, making sure to scrape the sides so all ingredients are combined.
2. Spread the bean salad on an open tortilla wrap. Layer with lettuce and sliced tomatoes. Wrap up and serve immediately. The remaining salad can be kept refrigerated in an airtight container for up to 3 days.

Tuna Salad Melt

This recipe is made with bread, but you could also wrap this tuna salad up in large lettuce leaves for a low-carbohydrate alternative.

SERVES 4

Ingredients

4 slices whole-grain bread

2 cans solid white tuna in water, rinsed and drained

1 tablespoon chopped fresh parsley

¼ cup minced red onion

¼ cup minced celery

1 teaspoon fresh lemon juice

2 tablespoons nonfat plain Greek yogurt

2 tablespoons mayonnaise

¼ teaspoon garlic powder

⅛ teaspoon ground black pepper

⅛ teaspoon ground sage

4 slices sharp Cheddar cheese

1 plum tomato, sliced

1. Preheat the broiler. Lightly toast the bread. Lay on a baking sheet.

2. Combine the tuna, parsley, onion, celery, lemon juice, Greek yogurt, mayonnaise, garlic powder, pepper, and sage in a medium bowl and mix well.

3. Spread the tuna mixture on each slice of bread. Top each slice with Cheddar cheese and sliced tomatoes. Place under the broiler for 2–3 minutes until the cheese is melted. Let cool on the baking sheet for 5 minutes before serving.

PER SERVING

Calories: 318

Fat: 13.5 g

Cholesterol: 66 mg

Carbohydrates: 18 g

Sugar: 9 g

Fiber: 2.25 g

Sodium: 725 mg

Protein: 31 g

DILL CHICKEN POTATO SALAD

Robin of *www.kneadtocook.com* shared this wonderful twist on classic potato salad. This can be made ahead of time and refrigerated until you're ready to serve.

SERVES 8

Ingredients

2 tablespoons extra-virgin olive oil

8 chicken tenders

½ teaspoon sea salt, divided use, or to taste

¼ teaspoon ground black pepper, divided use, or to taste

2 pounds red potatoes, scrubbed and cubed

2 tablespoons red wine vinegar

4 tablespoons nonfat plain Greek yogurt

2 tablespoons chopped fresh dill

½ English cucumber, cut lengthwise and chopped

1 red bell pepper, diced

1. In a large skillet, add the olive oil and heat for 1 minute. Add the chicken and season with salt and pepper. Cook until no longer pink, about 5–7 minutes. Remove from the skillet and refrigerate to cool.

2. In the meantime, get a large pot of salted water ready for the potatoes. Once at a rapid boil, add the potatoes and cook until fork-tender, about 10 minutes. Drain and let cool completely.

3. In a covered storage container, add the red wine vinegar, Greek yogurt, dill, and salt and pepper to taste. Cover and shake well. Refrigerate until needed.

4. Once all the items are properly cooled, cube the chicken and add it to a large bowl. Then add the cooled potatoes, cucumbers, and pepper, and dress with the Greek dill dressing. Gently stir to coat and top with salt and pepper.

PER SERVING

Calories: 199	Sugar: 3 g
Fat: 4 g	Fiber: 3 g
Cholesterol: 20 mg	Sodium: 251 mg
Carbohydrates: 28 g	Protein: 14 g

Grilled Pear Salad with Blue Cheese Vinaigrette

The flavors of this salad blend together perfectly—the sweet pears are irresistible when paired with tangy blue cheese. Try adding some lean chicken, turkey, or tuna to make this a more filling entrée.

(V) SERVES 6

Ingredients

3 Bosc or Bartlett pears, cut into 1½"-thick wedges

6 cups arugula

½ small onion, diced

2 cloves garlic, minced

½ cup extra-virgin olive oil

⅓ cup balsamic vinegar

1½ teaspoons turbinado sugar

½ teaspoon salt

4 tablespoons crumbled blue cheese

3 tablespoons nonfat plain Greek yogurt

2 tablespoons pecans

1. Preheat the grill to medium heat. With the grill lid covered, grill the pear wedges 1–2 minutes on each side until golden. Place the arugula in a large bowl and top with the onion and grilled pears.
2. Combine the garlic, olive oil, balsamic vinegar, sugar, salt, blue cheese, and Greek yogurt until thoroughly mixed. Pour the dressing over the arugula. Add the pecans and toss gently. Serve immediately.

PER SERVING

Calories: 265	Sugar: 11 g
Fat: 22 g	Fiber: 3 g
Cholesterol: 5 mg	Sodium: 282 mg
Carbohydrates: 18 g	Protein: 3 g

Waldorf Chicken Salad

This creamy classic salad is another fantastic recipe from my friend Carrie of *www.carriesexperimentalkitchen .blogspot.com*. Carrie lightens up the traditional version by adding Greek yogurt, which adds protein and a little tang. You can substitute plain Greek yogurt if you can't find the apple cinnamon flavor.

SERVES 8 (YIELDS 4 CUPS)

Ingredients

Dressing
½ cup mayonnaise

¼ cup nonfat apple cinnamon Greek yogurt

2 teaspoons honey

½ teaspoon kosher salt

Salad
2 cups diced cooked chicken

1–2 stalks celery, rinsed and chopped

½ cup chopped walnuts

1 apple, washed and cored

Juice from ½ lemon

1. To assemble the dressing: Add all the dressing ingredients to a small bowl, then whisk together until creamy. Refrigerate for 30 minutes before topping the salad.
2. To assemble the salad: In a medium bowl, add the chicken, celery, and walnuts.
3. Chop the apple into bite-size pieces and add to the chicken mixture.
4. Add the prepared dressing and lemon juice and mix well. Keep refrigerated, and serve cold.

PER SERVING (PER ½ CUP)

Calories: 197	Sugar: 6 g
Fat: 9.5 g	Fiber: 1 g
Cholesterol: 32 mg	Sodium: 333 mg
Carbohydrates: 12 g	Protein: 16 g

MEDITERRANEAN MACARONI SALAD

There's no need to wait for a picnic or barbecue to make this salad—it's perfect any time of year. If you're preparing the recipe in advance, reserve half of the dressing when tossing, and refrigerate. Add the reserved other half of the dressing right before serving.

Ⓥ SERVES 12

Ingredients

Dressing

1 cup low-fat plain Greek yogurt

Juice from 2 fresh lemons

½ teaspoon salt

¼ teaspoon ground black pepper

2 tablespoons extra-virgin olive oil

2 teaspoons apple cider vinegar

Salad

1 pound elbow macaroni

8 ounces baby spinach leaves, torn

1 pint grape tomatoes, halved

½ cup chopped red onion

1 (15-ounce) can chickpeas, drained and rinsed

1 (5-ounce) jar kalamata olives, pitted and halved

1 cucumber, halved and sliced

1. Whisk together the ingredients for dressing in a medium bowl. Set aside.
2. Cook the pasta according to package directions. Drain, and place in a large bowl.
3. Add the remaining ingredients to the large bowl. Mix together. Add the dressing to the pasta mixture and mix well. Refrigerate at least 2 hours before serving; it will taste better if the salad is refrigerated overnight to enhance the flavors. If refrigerating overnight, add half of the dressing right away and reserve the remaining half to add right before serving.

PER SERVING

Calories: 231	Sugar: 3 g
Fat: 4 g	Fiber: 3.6 g
Cholesterol: 1 mg	Sodium: 268 mg
Carbohydrates: 40 g	Protein: 9 g

CREAMY CAESAR SALAD WITH GARLIC CROUTONS

You won't miss the anchovies in this Caesar dressing—the Worcestershire sauce adds an incredible depth of flavor. Homemade garlic croutons add the perfect crunch and a gourmet touch. Grilled shrimp or chicken make delicious additions to this salad.

SERVES 6

Ingredients

Dressing
1 tablespoon lemon juice
1½ teaspoons Dijon mustard
1 tablespoon apple cider vinegar
2 cloves garlic
½ cup low-fat plain Greek yogurt
1 teaspoon Worcestershire sauce
½ teaspoon salt
¼ teaspoon ground black pepper
2 tablespoons freshly grated Parmesan cheese

Croutons
4 cups cubed French bread
3 tablespoons butter
3 cloves garlic, minced

Salad
1 head romaine lettuce, torn into bite-size pieces
4 tablespoons shaved fresh Parmesan cheese

1. In a blender or food processor, combine all ingredients for the dressing. Blend until smooth, and set aside.
2. Preheat the oven to 325°F. Place the bread on a baking sheet in a single layer.
3. In a skillet, add the butter and minced garlic and cook over medium heat for 2–3 minutes, until the butter melts and the garlic softens. Pour the butter mixture over the bread cubes on the baking sheet. Bake for 15–20 minutes until golden brown, making sure to turn a few times. Remove from oven and allow to cool.
4. Place the lettuce in a large bowl. Top with the shaved Parmesan cheese, croutons, and dressing. Toss and serve immediately.

PER SERVING

Calories: 228	Sugar: 2.5 g
Fat: 9 g	Fiber: 3.5 g
Cholesterol: 21 mg	Sodium: 622 mg
Carbohydrates: 28 g	Protein: 9 g

Spicy Grilled Corn and Bean Salad

This salad is perfect for an outdoor barbecue or a dinner party with friends. Fresh corn tastes best in this salad, and you can adjust the amount of seasonings to suit your taste.

V **SERVES 10**

Ingredients

4 ears fresh corn, husks removed

1 (15-ounce) can black or pinto beans, drained and rinsed

½ cup chopped green onion

1 large red bell pepper, diced

1 (4-ounce) can jalapeño peppers, diced

1 cup grape tomatoes, halved

¼ cup low-fat plain Greek yogurt

½ teaspoon chili powder

1 tablespoon fresh lime juice

1 teaspoon apple cider vinegar

1 tablespoon extra-virgin olive oil

2 tablespoons chopped fresh cilantro, divided use

1 clove garlic, minced

1 teaspoon salt

1. Preheat the grill to 375°F or to medium-high heat. Place the corn on the grill and cover grill lid. Grill for 15 minutes, making sure to turn over every 5 minutes for even cooking. Some kernels will char and blacken and may even pop. Cool slightly, then cut the kernels off the cobs. Discard the cobs.
2. In a large bowl, mix together the corn, beans, onion, peppers, and tomatoes.
3. In a small bowl, mix the Greek yogurt, chili powder, lime juice, vinegar, oil, 1 tablespoon cilantro, garlic, and salt until combined.
4. Pour the Greek yogurt mixture into the large bowl with the corn mixture and mix well. Refrigerate for at least 2 hours so the flavors can blend. (This salad can be refrigerated overnight.) Sprinkle the remaining tablespoon of cilantro over the top just before serving. Store refrigerated in an airtight container for up to 3 days.

PER SERVING

Calories: 118	Sugar: 3 g
Fat: 2 g	Fiber: 3.5 g
Cholesterol: 0 mg	Sodium: 251 mg
Carbohydrates: 21 g	Protein: 5.6 g

Spinach Salad with Creamy Avocado Dressing

Once you taste this salad you will want to make it over and over again! The dressing is simple to prepare, and will stay fresh in an airtight container in the refrigerator for up to 5 days.

V **SERVES 8**

Ingredients

Dressing

1 large ripe avocado, peeled and pitted

2 teaspoons fresh lemon juice

½ cup low-fat plain Greek yogurt

¼ cup extra-virgin olive oil

2 cloves garlic

½ teaspoon salt

1 teaspoon red wine vinegar

2 tablespoons chopped red onion

½ teaspoon Dijon mustard

Salad

10 ounces spinach, rinsed and torn into bite-size pieces

1 apple, peeled, cored, and chopped or 3 cups cubed watermelon or 1 pint strawberries, stems removed and chopped

½ cup walnuts

½ cup crumbled feta cheese

1. Place all ingredients for the dressing in a food processor or blender. Blend until smooth. Place in airtight container for at least 2 hours so the flavors can blend.
2. Place the spinach in a large bowl. Place the chopped fruit and walnuts on top. Add the cheese and dressing. Toss well, and serve immediately.

PER SERVING

Calories: 251	Sugar: 3 g
Fat: 21 g	Fiber: 4 g
Cholesterol: 9 mg	Sodium: 292 mg
Carbohydrates: 11.5 g	Protein: 7 g

SHRIMP SALAD

This is a delicious alternative to ordinary salads. This can be served over a bed of mixed greens or on bread as a sandwich. For a special treat, try toasting your Shrimp Salad on a panini press with crisp romaine or iceberg lettuce, sandwiched between slices of hearty whole-wheat bread.

SERVES 6

Ingredients

⅓ cup low-fat plain Greek yogurt

1 tablespoon fresh lemon juice

2 green onions, diced

½ teaspoon balsamic vinegar

¼ teaspoon ground paprika

1 clove garlic, minced

½ teaspoon salt

¼ teaspoon ground black pepper

1 pound large cooked shrimp, peeled and deveined, chopped

1 large ripe avocado, peeled and pitted, diced

1 large tomato, diced

¼ cup diced cucumber

1. In a medium bowl, mix together the Greek yogurt, lemon juice, onions, balsamic vinegar, paprika, garlic, salt, and pepper until well combined.
2. In a large bowl, add the chopped shrimp, avocado, tomato, and cucumber. Stir to combine. Add the Greek yogurt mixture and mix well. Cover and chill in refrigerator for at least 2 hours before serving.

PER SERVING

Calories: 154	Sugar: 3 g
Fat: 6 g	Fiber: 3.5 g
Cholesterol: 147 mg	Sodium: 373 mg
Carbohydrates: 6.5 g	Protein: 18.5 g

Quinoa-Avocado Salad with Cilantro Lime Dressing

This is a wonderful meatless dish that is packed with protein and vitamins. If you prepare this the night before, make sure to save a little dressing to toss through right before serving.

 SERVES 8

Ingredients

Salad
1½ cups uncooked quinoa, rinsed and drained

3 cups water

2 (15-ounce) cans black beans, rinsed and drained

1 (14-ounce) box frozen corn, defrosted

2 avocados, peeled and cut into ½" pieces

2 pints grape tomatoes, halved

Dressing
1 clove garlic, minced

3 tablespoons grapeseed oil

3 tablespoons nonfat plain Greek yogurt

¾ teaspoon minced fresh gingerroot

¼ cup fresh lime juice

Zest of 1 lime

2 teaspoons balsamic vinegar

¼ cup fresh packed cilantro leaves

Salt, to taste

1. Cook the quinoa in the water according to package directions. Let cool to room temperature.
2. In a medium bowl, combine the beans, corn, avocado, and tomatoes. Toss with the cooled quinoa.
3. Mix all ingredients for the dressing together in a small bowl. Refrigerate until ready to serve, for several hours or overnight, or immediately pour the dressing over the salad to serve.

PER SERVING

Calories: 479	Sugar: 6 g
Fat: 17 g	Fiber: 18 g
Cholesterol: 0 mg	Sodium: 19 mg
Carbohydrates: 70 g	Protein: 18 g

Chapter 8

PASTA

Good news—now you can enjoy your favorite pasta dishes and comfort foods, without the guilt! Greek yogurt makes a wonderful substitution for ricotta cheese and the creams typically found in pasta dishes. It has the same consistency and mild flavor that enhances these dishes, so you'll still have a creamy taste and texture—and still feel comforted and satisfied—without extra fat and calories. There are endless options when preparing pasta dishes, and Greek yogurt makes a great addition to them all. From Alfredo sauces to lasagna, and baked ziti to stuffed shells, the creamy pasta dishes typically considered to be unhealthy are transformed into dishes you can feel good about eating, and serving to your loved ones. As a bonus to you: if you're short on time, many of these sauces can be prepared ahead of time and kept refrigerated or frozen until you're ready to serve them. You will be astounded at how wonderfully mouthwatering your favorite pasta dishes turn out—and so will your friends and family.

Creamy Macaroni and Cheese with Bacon

This is classic comfort food at its finest. Children and adults both love this dish—and both will ask for a second helping.

SERVES 6

Ingredients

2 cups elbow macaroni

2 tablespoons butter

2 tablespoons flour

½ teaspoon salt

½ teaspoon ground black pepper

¼ cup nonfat plain Greek yogurt

1½ cups fat-free milk

1 cup shredded Cheddar cheese

5 ounces shredded fontina or Gruyère cheese

1 tablespoon bread crumbs

1 tablespoon grated Parmesan cheese

4 slices uncured, center-cut bacon, cooked

PER SERVING

Calories: 412	Sugar: 4 g
Fat: 10 g	Fiber: 1.5 g
Cholesterol: 65 mg	Sodium: 716 mg
Carbohydrates: 34 g	Protein: 21 g

1. Preheat the oven to 400°F. Butter a 1½-quart casserole or baking dish.
2. In a medium saucepan, cook the pasta until al dente, about 6 minutes. Drain and set aside.
3. In a separate saucepan, melt the butter over medium heat. Slowly add in the flour, salt, and pepper. Mix well until smooth.
4. Slowly add the Greek yogurt and milk, continuing to stir to make sure the sauce is smooth. Add the cheeses; continue to stir until the cheese is melted and the sauce is thickened.
5. In a large bowl, add the cheese sauce to the drained pasta. Stir to coat. Pour into the prepared baking dish. Sprinkle the bread crumbs, Parmesan cheese, and crumbled bacon on top.
6. Bake for 20–25 minutes until the bread crumbs are browned and the sauce is bubbly.

KALE AND WHITE BEAN BAKED PASTA

This is a wonderful way to mix up your pasta recipes. The Greek yogurt and beans add protein to this tasty meatless dish.

Ⓥ SERVES 6

Ingredients

1 pound penne pasta

1 tablespoon extra-virgin olive oil

3 cloves garlic, minced

½ cup diced onion

1 cup cleaned, chopped baby bella mushrooms, stems removed

5 cups trimmed and chopped kale

1 (15-ounce) can white cannellini beans, drained and rinsed

½ cup plus 1 tablespoon freshly grated Parmesan cheese, divided use

1 cup shredded mozzarella

¾ cup nonfat plain Greek yogurt

1 teaspoon fresh lemon juice

1 tablespoon bread crumbs

1. Preheat the oven to 350°F.
2. In a large pot, cook the pasta until al dente, according to package directions. Drain, and set aside.
3. In a large skillet, heat the oil over medium heat. Sauté the garlic and onion for 2–3 minutes until soft. Add the mushrooms and stir. Cook for another 2 minutes. Add the kale and cook for 3–4 minutes until the kale is wilted and bright green. Add the beans and mix well. Turn the heat to low and simmer for another 3–4 minutes.
4. In a medium bowl, mix ½ cup Parmesan, mozzarella, Greek yogurt, and lemon juice. Mix in the pasta. Slowly add the kale mixture and mix well. Pour into a 2½-quart casserole dish. Top with the bread crumbs and remaining Parmesan. Bake for 15–20 minutes until golden brown. Serve immediately.

PER SERVING

Calories: 522	Sugar: 3 g
Fat: 10.5 g	Fiber: 10 g
Cholesterol: 18 mg	Sodium: 270 mg
Carbohydrates: 80 g	Protein: 28 g

Shrimp and Spinach Pasta Medley

Crusty French bread would pair perfectly with this pasta dish. The cream sauce is full of flavor and light enough that you won't feel guilty about having a second serving.

SERVES 6

Ingredients

1 (12-ounce) box linguine
2 tablespoons butter, divided use
12 ounces shrimp, deveined, tails removed
2 cloves garlic, minced
½ medium onion, minced
3 cups torn spinach
1 red bell pepper, chopped
½ cup low-fat plain Greek yogurt
2 tablespoons fresh lemon juice
½ cup grated Parmesan cheese, plus more for topping
1 teaspoon garlic powder

PER SERVING

Calories: 371
Fat: 8 g
Cholesterol: 129 mg
Carbohydrates: 48 g
Sugar: 3 g
Fiber: 1 g
Sodium: 303 mg
Protein: 25 g

1. Cook the linguine according to package directions. Drain, rinse, and set aside.
2. In a large skillet, cook 1 tablespoon butter over medium heat for 1 minute until melted. Add the shrimp and cook 2–3 minutes on both sides until pink. Using tongs, remove the shrimp and place in a medium bowl. Place a paper towel on top of the bowl to keep the shrimp warm.
3. In the same skillet, melt 1 tablespoon butter over medium heat. Add the garlic and onion and cook for 2–3 minutes until soft. Add the spinach and pepper and cook for 3–4 minutes until the spinach is wilted and the pepper is soft. Add the shrimp and linguine to the skillet and stir. Remove from heat.
4. In a small bowl, mix together the Greek yogurt, lemon juice, ½ cup Parmesan cheese, and garlic powder until combined. Add the Greek yogurt mixture to the skillet and mix thoroughly so it is well combined. Top with extra Parmesan cheese, if desired. Serve immediately.

Classic Baked Ziti

This dish can be prepared in advance and placed in the refrigerator until you are ready to eat. You don't have to layer the ingredients as posted in the instructions, but it does make for a prettier presentation. You can simply mix the cheeses, meat, and sauce together and bake.

SERVES 8

Ingredients

1 pound ziti pasta

1 pound lean ground turkey

1 tablespoon olive oil

1 medium onion, chopped

2 cloves garlic, minced

1 (28-ounce) can crushed tomatoes

1 (15-ounce) can tomato sauce

1 teaspoon ground basil

1 teaspoon ground oregano

½ teaspoon salt

½ teaspoon ground black pepper

1 cup ricotta cheese

1 cup nonfat plain Greek yogurt

½ cup shredded mozzarella cheese, divided use

1 tablespoon grated Parmesan cheese

PER SERVING

Calories: 424	Sugar: 4 g
Fat: 8 g	Fiber: 11 g
Cholesterol: 38 mg	Sodium: 734 mg
Carbohydrates: 63 g	Protein: 28.5 g

1. Preheat the oven to 350°F.
2. Bring a large pot of water to a boil, add pasta, and cook for 7 minutes until al dente.
3. In a medium skillet, add the ground turkey. Cook for 15 minutes until no longer pink and thoroughly cooked. Set aside.
4. In a large skillet, add the oil. Cook the onion and garlic over medium-high heat for 3–4 minutes until soft. Add crushed tomatoes, tomato sauce, basil, oregano, salt, and pepper. Stir well and bring to a boil. Reduce heat to low and simmer for 15 minutes, making sure to stir every few minutes so the sauce doesn't stick. Spoon some sauce into a 2½-quart casserole dish so the bottom is covered (to ensure the pasta won't stick to the bottom). Take 1 cup of sauce mixture and set aside. Spoon the meat into the remaining sauce.
5. In a medium bowl, mix together the ricotta and Greek yogurt until combined. Spoon half of the ricotta mixture on top of the sauce in the casserole dish. Sprinkle ¼ cup mozzarella cheese, then layer with half the pasta. Pour half of the meat sauce on top, then layer with the rest of the ricotta mixture and the remaining mozzarella. Add the rest of the pasta and the remaining meat sauce. Sprinkle the top with Parmesan cheese.
6. Cover loosely with aluminum foil to prevent drying and bake for 15 minutes. Remove the aluminum foil and continue to bake another 10 minutes until the cheese has melted. Let sit for 10 minutes, and serve with the reserved cup of sauce.

Roasted Spaghetti Squash with Creamy Pesto Sauce

Spaghetti squash makes a wonderful low-carbohydrate alternative to pasta. Its mild taste pairs well with the bold flavors of basil pesto in this dish.

 SERVES 4

Ingredients

1 (3½–4 pound) spaghetti squash

2 cloves garlic, minced

2 tablespoons plus ½ cup extra-virgin olive oil, divided use

¼ teaspoon salt

¼ teaspoon ground black pepper

3 cloves garlic, left whole

3 tablespoons pine nuts

¼ cup Parmesan cheese

2 ounces fresh basil leaves, torn

½ cup nonfat plain Greek yogurt

PER SERVING

Calories: 261	Sugar: 9 g
Fat: 16 g	Fiber: 6 g
Cholesterol: 7 mg	Sodium: 315 mg
Carbohydrates: 25 g	Protein: 9 g

1. Preheat the oven to 375°F.
2. Cut the spaghetti squash in half lengthwise with a sharp knife. Scoop out the seeds and discard. Place the squash halves into a large casserole dish face up.
3. In a small bowl, mix the minced garlic, 2 tablespoons oil, salt, and pepper. Spread the oil mixture on each half of the squash.
4. Bake for 40 minutes. Let the squash completely cool for 20–30 minutes.
5. While the squash is cooling, add ½ cup oil, 3 whole cloves garlic, pine nuts, Parmesan cheese, basil, and Greek yogurt to a food processor or high-powered blender in the order listed. Blend for 2–3 minutes, until smooth.
6. Using a fork, scoop and separate the squash strands until all the squash is out. Place the strands in a bowl or on a plate, and place the creamy pesto sauce on top of the spaghetti squash in spoonfuls. Serve the remaining sauce on the side for dipping.

Microwave Your Squash!

Low on time? You can also "roast" your spaghetti squash in the microwave! Using a sharp knife, pierce the squash all over to prevent the squash from bursting. Place face up on a microwaveable plate, and pour the oil mixture on each half. Cook in an 800-watt microwave on high for 6–7 minutes. Turn it over, and cook an additional 8–9 minutes until the squash is soft. Let the squash cool before serving.

Seafood Fettuccine Alfredo

This is a perfect example of how easily you can lighten up a dish that is normally loaded with fat and calories. The Greek yogurt adds protein and a wonderful thick texture.

SERVES 8

Ingredients

1 pound fettuccine

1 tablespoon butter

1 teaspoon fresh lemon juice

5 cloves garlic, minced

½ cup chopped onion

1 pound seafood mixture of your choice (such as frozen shrimp, calamari, and bay scallops)

¾ cup half-and-half

½ cup nonfat plain Greek yogurt

½ teaspoon salt

¼ teaspoon ground black pepper

⅓ cup freshly grated Parmesan cheese

Fresh parsley, for garnish

1. Cook fettuccine according to package directions. Drain and set aside.
2. In a large skillet, sauté the butter, lemon juice, garlic, and onion over medium heat for 3 minutes until soft. Add the seafood and cook for 3–4 minutes until the shrimp is pink, and the scallops and calamari are opaque. Remove from heat.
3. In a medium bowl, mix together the half and half, Greek yogurt, salt, and pepper until smooth. Add the Parmesan cheese, and pour into the skillet with the seafood. Mix well. Let sit for 5 minutes and allow the sauce to thicken. Slowly add the cooked fettuccine and mix thoroughly. Garnish with fresh parsley to serve.

PER SERVING

Calories: 352	Sugar: 2 g
Fat: 7 g	Fiber: 3 g
Cholesterol: 127 mg	Sodium: 687 mg
Carbohydrates: 46 g	Protein: 24 g

Mushroom and Pancetta Stuffed Shells

This classic Italian dish has a zesty cheese sauce that is sure to please your family and friends. Try serving it with a fresh arugula salad and a light lemon vinaigrette.

SERVES 10

Ingredients

12 ounces jumbo pasta shells

1 tablespoon extra-virgin olive oil

2 cloves garlic, minced

¼ pound thick pancetta, diced

2 cups cleaned, diced baby bella mushrooms, stems removed

2 eggs

15 ounces ricotta cheese

2 cups nonfat plain Greek yogurt

3 tablespoons diced fresh parsley

2 tablespoons diced fresh basil

½ cup Parmesan cheese, divided use

5 cups pasta sauce

¼ cup shredded mozzarella cheese

PER SERVING

Calories: 369	Sugar: 9 g
Fat: 12 g	Fiber: 2 g
Cholesterol: 72 mg	Sodium: 781 mg
Carbohydrates: 41 g	Protein: 23 g

1. Preheat the oven to 350°F.
2. Bring a large pot of water to a boil. Add the pasta shells and cook until al dente, about 8 minutes. Set aside.
3. In a large skillet, add the olive oil and garlic. Sauté over medium heat for 1–2 minutes until soft. Add the pancetta and cook for 3 minutes until slightly browned. Add the mushrooms and cook for another 2–3 minutes until they soften. Remove from heat.
4. In a large bowl, combine the eggs, ricotta, Greek yogurt, parsley, basil, ¼ cup Parmesan, and half of the mushroom/pancetta mixture. Mix well. Pour 1 cup of pasta sauce on the bottom of a 9" × 13" baking dish.
5. Stuff each shell with cheese mixture and place in the baking dish. Pour the remaining sauce on top of the shells. Top with the remaining mushroom/pancetta mixture. Sprinkle with the remaining ¼ cup Parmesan and mozzarella.
6. Bake for 45 minutes until the edges are bubbly.

Choosing Fresh or Dried Herbs

If you don't have fresh herbs, don't worry. You can easily substitute dried seasonings instead. You need 3 times the amount of fresh herbs to equal the amount of dried. One tablespoon of fresh herbs equals 1 teaspoon dried, since 1 tablespoon equals 3 teaspoons. Be sure to remember this ratio when cooking, so you don't overpower your dishes with too much dried seasoning!

ROASTED EGGPLANT AND TURKEY SAUSAGE PASTA

Keep the peel on your eggplant to add color and fiber to this wonderful dish. You can use whatever kind of turkey sausage you like in this recipe.

SERVES 6

Ingredients

1 medium eggplant
½ teaspoon salt
3 tablespoons extra-virgin olive oil, divided use
1 pound pasta
1 pound nitrate-free, reduced-fat turkey sausage
2 cloves garlic, diced
1 teaspoon dried basil
1 teaspoon dried oregano
¼ teaspoon dried thyme
⅛ teaspoon crushed red pepper flakes
1 (15-ounce) can diced tomatoes
¼ cup nonfat plain Greek yogurt
¼ cup grated Romano cheese
2 tablespoons chopped fresh parsley

PER SERVING

Calories: 514
Fat: 19 g
Cholesterol: 53 mg
Carbohydrates: 67 g
Sugar: 3 g
Fiber: 11 g
Sodium: 774 mg
Protein: 23 g

1. Slice the eggplant into rounds. Place in a colander and sprinkle salt all over. Allow the eggplant to sit for 1 hour to remove moisture and bitterness. Rinse under cold water and pat dry with paper towels. Cut into cubes.
2. Preheat the oven to 400°F. Place the eggplant in a baking dish and coat with 2 tablespoons olive oil. Toss to combine. Bake for 25 minutes, making sure to stir at least once. Set aside.
3. Cook the pasta according to package directions. Drain and set aside.
4. In a large skillet, cook the sausage with the remaining tablespoon olive oil over medium heat. Cook until no longer pink, about 10–12 minutes. Slice sausage into 1" pieces. Add the garlic, basil, oregano, thyme, red pepper flakes, and tomatoes. Stir well and lower heat. Simmer for 3–4 minutes. Pour the sausage mixture into a large bowl. Add the cooked pasta and eggplant, and stir to combine. Add the Greek yogurt and mix well. Top with Romano cheese and parsley. Serve immediately.

Sausage Safety Tips

All sausages are not the same. Many people choose to eat turkey or chicken sausage as a "healthy" substitute for pork. It can be, but you must read your labels. Look for ones that are "nitrite free," which means they don't contain cancer-causing chemicals that are added to foods as flavor enhancers. Also, read ingredient labels to avoid MSG (monosodium glutamate), which is a highly concentrated salt that is also added to foods to improve flavor.

Scallops and Sun-Dried Tomatoes over Penne

These sumptuous scallops will melt in your mouth. The sweetness of the scallops and the tang of the wine sauce create an explosion of flavor. You can substitute chicken or shrimp for the scallops if you'd like.

SERVES 6

Ingredients

1 pound box whole-grain penne pasta

2 tablespoons butter

¾ pound small scallops

3 cloves garlic, minced

¼ cup diced onion

¼ cup diced sun-dried tomatoes

1 cup dry white wine

2 tablespoons minced fresh parsley

½ cup nonfat plain Greek yogurt

2 tablespoons capers

PER SERVING

Calories: 378

Fat: 5.5 g

Cholesterol: 29 mg

Carbohydrates: 58 g

Sugar: 4 g

Fiber: 3 g

Sodium: 503 mg

Protein: 21 g

1. In a large pot of boiling water, cook the penne for 8 minutes or until al dente. Drain and set aside.
2. In a large skillet, melt the butter over medium-high heat. Sauté the scallops for 2–3 minutes on each side until opaque. With a slotted spoon, transfer the scallops to a plate. Add the garlic, onion, and sun-dried tomatoes to the skillet and sauté in the remaining butter sauce for 3–4 minutes until soft. Add wine and parsley and cook another 1–2 minutes. Remove from heat.
3. Add the Greek yogurt to the wine mixture and stir well. Add the scallops and stir to combine. In a large bowl, pour the scallop mixture over the penne. Toss with capers. Serve immediately.

Linguine with Roasted Red Pepper Sauce

Your guests will never believe that this creamy sauce isn't loaded with fat and calories. There is no need for cream in this delicious sauce; Greek yogurt adds enough creaminess without all the saturated fat.

 SERVES 8

Ingredients

2 large red bell peppers

Olive oil, for coating peppers, plus 2 tablespoons

4 cloves garlic, chopped

¼ cup chopped onion

1 tablespoon dried basil

2 cups nonfat plain Greek yogurt

⅓ cup shredded Asiago cheese

1 pound cooked linguine

PER SERVING

Calories: 153	Sugar: 4 g
Fat: 5.5 g	Fiber: 1 g
Cholesterol: 8 mg	Sodium: 90 mg
Carbohydrates: 16 g	Protein: 9.5 g

1. Preheat the broiler. Lightly coat peppers with olive oil and place on a baking sheet. Place in the oven and broil for about 15 minutes, making sure to turn over halfway, until the peppers turn black and charred.

2. Carefully remove peppers from the oven and place in a large bowl. Cover tightly with plastic wrap, making sure that it's sealed airtight. Let sit for 15 minutes to help loosen the skins.

3. Pull the stems out of the peppers and peel the skins off. This should be relatively simple to do. Lift each pepper with one hand, and use your other hand to push down on the pepper. The seeds and white flesh should squeeze out. Scrape out any remaining seeds or ribs.

4. Chop the peppers into small pieces.

5. Add 2 tablespoons oil to a large saucepan, and heat to medium-high. Sauté the garlic, onion, and basil for about 2 minutes until somewhat softened. Add the chopped peppers, and cook for 8–10 minutes until completely softened.

6. Place Greek yogurt and red pepper mixture in a blender or food processor, and blend until it reaches the desired consistency. Pour this mixture back into the saucepan. Add cheese, and stir until completely melted.

7. Pour sauce over cooked linguine. Serve immediately.

Red Pepper Shortcut

Do you need to save preparation time? Jarred roasted red peppers are a quick and convenient option for this dish. Just be sure to drain all oil from the peppers before adding to the saucepan.

Buffalo Chicken Pasta

You will feel like you are eating your favorite chicken wings when you eat this salad, but without the sticky fingers! Tangy and cool Gorgonzola cheese tops this irresistible dish, and balances the spice from the hot sauce.

SERVES 6

Ingredients

1 pound pasta

3 chicken breasts, cooked and cubed (about 5 ounces each)

2 stalks celery, diced

3 tablespoons hot sauce

¼ cup low-fat plain Greek yogurt

½ cup Gorgonzola cheese

¾ cup chopped green onions

1. Cook the pasta according to package directions. Rinse and drain. Pour into a large bowl. Place the chopped chicken and celery in the bowl with the pasta.
2. In a small bowl, mix together the hot sauce and Greek yogurt until combined. Pour over the pasta and chicken and mix well.
3. Top with the Gorgonzola cheese and green onions. Serve immediately.

PER SERVING

Calories: 394	Sugar: 2 g
Fat: 6 g	Fiber: 3 g
Cholesterol: 49 mg	Sodium: 264 mg
Carbohydrates: 55 g	Protein: 29 g

Spinach and Feta Cheese Gnocchi

This simple pasta dish will be a favorite of yours for years to come. Feta and Greek yogurt combine perfectly to make this wonderful, creamy sauce. Feel free to add cooked chopped chicken for some extra protein.

 SERVES 8

Ingredients

12 ounces gnocchi
2 tablespoons extra-virgin olive oil
2 cloves garlic, minced
1 cup sliced mushrooms
10 ounces fresh baby spinach
1 cup chopped tomatoes
⅛ teaspoon red pepper flakes
½ teaspoon salt
¼ teaspoon ground black pepper
½ cup low-fat plain Greek yogurt
⅓ cup crumbled feta cheese
2 tablespoons chopped fresh parsley, for topping

1. Cook the gnocchi according to package directions. Drain and place in a large bowl.
2. Heat a large skillet over medium heat. Add the oil and garlic and cook for 2–3 minutes until soft. Add mushrooms, spinach, tomatoes, red pepper flakes, salt, and pepper and cook until the spinach is wilted and the mushrooms are tender, about 5 minutes. Remove from heat and add to the large bowl of gnocchi.
3. In a small bowl, mix together the Greek yogurt and feta cheese. Pour the mixture over the gnocchi and vegetables, and stir to combine. Top with fresh parsley and serve immediately.

PER SERVING

Calories: 138	Sugar: 2 g
Fat: 6 g	Fiber: 2 g
Cholesterol: 6 mg	Sodium: 500 mg
Carbohydrates: 17 g	Protein: 5 g

Top: Mexican Quinoa Stuffed Peppers, *Chapter 6*
Bottom right: Carrot Ginger Apple Smoothie, *Chapter 4*
Bottom left: Amazing Apple Cinnamon Quinoa, *Chapter 2*

Top left: Grilled Pear Salad with Blue Cheese Vinaigrette, *Chapter 7*
Top right: Creamed Spinach, *Chapter 6*
Middle right: Tomato Asparagus Bean Medley, *Chapter 6*
Bottom: Avocado Egg Salad, *Chapter 7*

Top: Roasted Vegetable Tart, *Chapter 3*
Bottom: Fruit Kebabs with Yogurt Dipping Sauce, *Chapter 9*

Top left: Oatmeal Pancakes, *Chapter 2*
Top right: Strawberries and Cream Frozen Yogurt, *Chapter 9*
Bottom: Summer Cucumber Soup, *Chapter 3*

Top: Skillet Taco Quinoa, *Chapter 5*
Bottom right: Flax Berry Smoothie, *Chapter 4*
Bottom left: Curried Chicken Salad, *Chapter 7*

Top: Deviled Eggs , *Chapter 3*
Bottom right: Lemon Orzo with Toasted Pine Nuts , *Chapter 6*
Bottom left: Pumpkin Oatmeal Cookies, *Chapter 9*

Top left: Classic Baked Ziti, *Chapter 8*
Top right: Green with Envy Smoothie, *Chapter 4*
Bottom: Lemon Yogurt and Basil Chicken
Kebabs, *Chapter 5*

Top: Spinach and Feta Cheese Gnocchi, *Chapter 8*
Bottom right: Creamy Vegetable Quinoa Soup, *Chapter 3*
Bottom left: Banana Oatmeal, *Chapter 2*

Terrific Turkey Lasagna

This isn't your mother's ordinary lasagna. This hearty recipe is packed with meat, and the Greek yogurt adds a smooth, rich texture. You could easily use no-boil lasagna noodles to save time.

SERVES 12

Ingredients

1 (8-ounce) package lasagna noodles

2 tablespoons extra-virgin olive oil

2 cloves garlic, minced

½ cup chopped onion

1 pound lean, nitrate-free turkey sausage, sliced

1 pound ground turkey

1 (28-ounce) can crushed tomatoes

2 (6.5-ounce) cans tomato sauce

1 teaspoon dried basil

1 teaspoon dried oregano

1 teaspoon salt

¼ teaspoon ground black pepper

½ teaspoon turbinado sugar

1 egg

1 cup low-fat plain Greek yogurt

1 cup ricotta cheese

½ cup grated Parmesan cheese

1 cup shredded mozzarella cheese, divided use

PER SERVING

Calories: 304

Fat: 11 g

Cholesterol: 61 mg

Carbohydrates: 27 g

Sugar: 3 g

Fiber: 2 g

Sodium: 761 mg

Protein: 25 g

1. Bring a large pot of water to a rolling boil over high heat. Add the lasagna noodles and return to a boil. Cook uncovered, stirring occasionally, until the pasta is al dente, about 8 minutes. Drain and set aside.

2. In a large pot or Dutch oven, add the oil. Sauté the garlic and onion for 3–4 minutes over medium heat until softened. Add the sausage and ground turkey and cook for 5–7 minutes until no longer pink. Add the crushed tomatoes, tomato sauce, basil, oregano, salt, pepper, and sugar and bring to a boil. Reduce the heat to medium-low and simmer for 20 minutes, stirring occasionally.

3. In a medium bowl, mix together the egg, Greek yogurt, ricotta, Parmesan, and half of the shredded mozzarella.

4. Preheat the oven to 375°F. Spread a thin layer of the meat mixture on the bottom of a 9" × 13" casserole dish. Layer with ⅓ of the noodles. Spread ⅓ of the Greek yogurt mixture on top of the noodles, then top with another ⅓ of the meat sauce. Layer 2 more times, or until all the ingredients are used. Top with the remaining mozzarella cheese. Place aluminum foil loosely on top, being careful it doesn't touch the cheese. Bake for 25 minutes. Remove the foil and bake for an additional 25 minutes. Allow to cool for 15 minutes before serving.

Chapter 9

DESSERTS

Let's face it: desserts have a bad reputation. Commonly known as "diet saboteurs," desserts are typically loaded with extra fat and calories. Oil and butter are commonly used ingredients in many baked goods. They add texture, moisture, and subtle flavor to many of your favorite desserts. Unfortunately, they also add saturated fat, cholesterol, and extra calories. We all know that by constantly indulging in these fat-laden goodies, our waistlines get larger and our pants start to shrink. But how many times have you deprived yourself of enjoying a luscious piece of cheesecake or a chocolate chip cookie? More often than not, we tell ourselves "I shouldn't" when it's time for dessert. But now, thanks to Greek yogurt, you can enjoy dessert again—and many more decadent sweet treats—because it is the perfect low-fat, calcium-rich, and high-protein substitute for the typical fattening ingredients! The possibilities are endless, and this chapter will show you how to use Greek yogurt in incredibly mouthwatering desserts. From cookies to cakes, to sweet dips and frostings, Greek yogurt works perfectly every time. Now you really can have your cake and eat it too!

FRUIT KEBABS WITH YOGURT DIPPING SAUCE

This makes a wonderful afternoon snack for the kids, or a late afternoon treat for yourself. The protein in the Greek yogurt dip and fiber and nutrients in the fruit make a well-balanced snack that's as healthy as it is delicious. For a more decadent treat, try serving melted chocolate or a nut butter alongside the yogurt dip.

 YIELDS 6 KEBABS AND 2 CUPS DIPPING SAUCE

Ingredients

Kebabs

1 (16-ounce) container strawberries, sliced

1 kiwi, peeled and sliced

¼ cantaloupe, fruit scooped out with a melon baller

1 apple, cut into squares

¼ honeydew, fruit scooped out with a melon baller

Juice of ½ lemon

Dipping Sauce

2 cups nonfat vanilla Greek yogurt

½ cup honey

¼ teaspoon lemon juice

½ teaspoon ground cinnamon

1. Place sliced fruit in any order on skewers.
2. Sprinkle with fresh lemon juice to ensure the fruit stays fresh.
3. Mix all the ingredients for dipping sauce together in a small bowl. Serve immediately, or store covered in the refrigerator until ready to serve.

PER SERVING, WITH ⅓ CUP SAUCE

Calories: 201	Sugar: 14 g
Fat: 0.5 g	Fiber: 3 g
Cholesterol: 0 mg	Sodium: 39 mg
Carbohydrates: 44 g	Protein: 8 g

GREEN TEA KIWI POPSICLES

These are a wonderful twist on ordinary popsicles. If you make them for children, make sure to use decaffeinated green tea matcha powder.

 YIELDS 4 POPSICLES

Ingredients

1½ teaspoons green tea matcha powder

1 tablespoon boiling water

2 kiwis, peeled and diced

1½ cups low-fat vanilla Greek yogurt

1 teaspoon fresh lemon juice

3 tablespoons honey

PER SERVING

Calories: 141	Sugar: 7 g
Fat: 2 g	Fiber: 1.5 g
Cholesterol: 0 mg	Sodium: 37 mg
Carbohydrates: 23 g	Protein: 9.5 g

1. In a small bowl, combine the matcha powder and boiling water. Stir to combine to create a smooth paste. Set aside.
2. In a large bowl, mix the diced kiwis, Greek yogurt, lemon juice, and honey. Stir in the matcha paste, and make sure it is thoroughly combined.
3. Spoon the mixture into popsicle molds, making sure to only fill ¾ of the way up. Place popsicle sticks in the center of the popsicles. Place in the freezer until frozen.

Powerful Green Tea Matcha Powder

Not sure what green tea matcha powder is? It is a Japanese powdered green tea that can be used in drinks or as an ingredient in recipes. Green tea is packed with antioxidants that help fight dangerous free radicals in the body, which can cause disease and illness. Studies also show that green tea can help speed up your metabolism, which helps burn fat. You can purchase green tea matcha powder in Asian stores and specialty grocery stores online.

ALMOND DELIGHT YOGURT DIP

This delicious dip can be served with sliced fruits, vegetables, pretzels, chips, graham crackers, or even pancakes and waffles!

 SERVES 4

Ingredients

4 tablespoons almond butter
2 cups nonfat vanilla Greek yogurt
½ teaspoon ground cinnamon
1 tablespoon honey
½ teaspoon pure vanilla extract
¼ cup chocolate chips, for garnish

PER SERVING

Calories: 287
Fat: 13 g
Cholesterol: 0 mg
Carbohydrates: 29 g

Sugar: 23 g
Fiber: 2 g
Sodium: 53 mg
Protein: 14 g

1. Place all ingredients except chocolate chips in a medium bowl and mix well.
2. Serve with sliced fruits and vegetables immediately. Top with chocolate chips, if desired.

Strawberries and Cream Frozen Yogurt

This light dessert can be prepared with or without an ice cream machine. You can easily use frozen strawberries; just defrost them right before you mix them in with the Greek yogurt.

 SERVES 14

Ingredients
¾ cup fat-free milk
¼ cup turbinado sugar
4 cups low-fat vanilla Greek yogurt
2 cups strawberries, puréed

PER SERVING

Calories: 77	Sugar: 8 g
Fat: 1.5 g	Fiber: 0.5 g
Cholesterol: 4 mg	Sodium: 34 mg
Carbohydrates: 9 g	Protein: 7 g

1. In a medium bowl, mix the milk and sugar until the sugar is dissolved, about 1–2 minutes on low speed.
2. Stir in the Greek yogurt and strawberry purée.
3. If using an ice cream maker, freeze according to manufacturer's instructions. You can spoon the frozen yogurt into a tall, upright plastic container to place in the freezer.
4. If not using an ice cream maker, place all ingredients in a large bowl and mix well. Transfer to a shallow freezer-safe container with a lid. Seal tightly, and place in the freezer for 30 minutes. Take out and stir with a fork, and place back in the freezer until solid. Repeat this every 30 minutes or so, stirring vigorously to break up the ice crystals, until yogurt is well frozen. Allow to sit at room temperature for 5 minutes before serving. Store in airtight container for up to 1 week.

Beware of Store-Bought Frozen Yogurt
Store-bought frozen yogurt and ice creams may have over twenty ingredients in them! This recipe is a perfect example of how easy it is to make your own frozen yogurt at home with only 4 ingredients. Those added chemicals and preservatives are unnecessary and offer no nutritional benefits at all.

HEAVENLY CHEESECAKE

This wonderful classic dessert is lightened up a bit with Greek yogurt. Fresh berries add a pop of flavor that complements the creamy cake; try a combination of raspberries, strawberries, blueberries, or blackberries for natural sweetness and a burst of antioxidants.

Ⓥ SERVES 8

Ingredients

1 cup graham cracker crumbs or cookie crumbs

½ cup butter, melted

¼ teaspoon ground cinnamon

1 tablespoon plus ¾ cup turbinado sugar, divided use

1 (8-ounce) package cream cheese

1 cup nonfat plain Greek yogurt

1 tablespoon pure vanilla extract

1 tablespoon fresh lemon juice (about ½ medium lemon's worth)

2 eggs

Sliced fresh berries, for topping

PER SERVING

Calories: 347	Sugar: 28 g
Fat: 19.5 g	Fiber: 1 g
Cholesterol: 95 mg	Sodium: 358 mg
Carbohydrates: 36 g	Protein: 8.5 g

1. Preheat the oven to 325°F. Grease a 9" pie pan and set aside.
2. In a small bowl, mix together graham cracker or cookie crumbs, butter, cinnamon, and 1 tablespoon sugar. Press the mixture into the prepared pie pan, making sure to press evenly on the bottom and the sides of pan. Bake for 10 minutes.
3. Mix the cream cheese, Greek yogurt, remaining sugar, vanilla extract, and lemon juice in a medium bowl with an electric mixer on medium speed. When the mixture is almost smooth, add the eggs, one at time, on low speed. Continue to beat on low speed until smooth. Pour into the pie pan and bake for 60 minutes until the edges are golden brown. The middle will not be completely set. Cool on the counter for at least 30 minutes, and refrigerate for at least 4 hours or overnight. Top with fresh berries if desired. Serve cold.

COFFEE CAKE

This light cake can be served for breakfast or brunch with coffee or tea, or with a big glass of milk for dessert!

 SERVES 12

Ingredients

¾ cup melted salted butter

1 cup turbinado sugar

2 whole eggs

1 cup nonfat vanilla Greek yogurt

1 cup whole-wheat pastry flour

1 cup all-purpose flour

1 teaspoon baking powder

1 teaspoon baking soda

¾ cup packed brown sugar

1½ teaspoons ground cinnamon

PER SERVING

Calories: 335	Sugar: 33 g
Fat: 13 g	Fiber: 2 g
Cholesterol: 66 mg	Sodium: 269 mg
Carbohydrates: 50 g	Protein: 5 g

1. Preheat the oven to 350°F. Grease and flour a 10" Bundt pan.
2. With a mixer, beat the melted butter and turbinado sugar in a large bowl for about 2–3 minutes until fluffy.
3. With the mixer, beat the eggs and Greek yogurt into the sugar mixture until smooth.
4. In a separate medium bowl, mix the flours, baking powder, and baking soda until thoroughly combined. Stir the mixture into the Greek yogurt combination until a batter is formed.
5. In a small bowl, mix the brown sugar and cinnamon together.
6. Pour half of the batter into the prepared Bundt pan. Sprinkle half of the cinnamon sugar mixture on top of the batter. Pour the remaining batter on top. Sprinkle the remainder of the cinnamon mixture on top of the batter.
7. Bake for 35–40 minutes, or until a toothpick placed in the center comes out clean.

Pumpkin Oatmeal Cookies

Pumpkin cookies can be eaten any time of the year, not just in the fall. Top them with Cinnamon Yogurt Frosting (see recipe in this chapter), or serve them plain with a tall glass of milk.

 YIELDS 2½ DOZEN COOKIES

Ingredients

1 cup oats

1 cup all-purpose flour

¼ cup ground flaxseed (or flax meal)

½ teaspoon baking powder

¼ teaspoon baking soda

½ teaspoon pumpkin pie spice

½ teaspoon ground cinnamon

⅛ teaspoon salt

5 tablespoons butter, at room temperature

⅓ cup packed brown sugar

1 cup 100 percent pumpkin (not pumpkin pie filling)

½ cup nonfat vanilla Greek yogurt

1 large egg, beaten

1. Preheat the oven to 350°F. Set aside 2 nonstick baking sheets.
2. In a medium bowl, combine the oats, flour, flaxseed, baking powder, baking soda, pumpkin pie spice, cinnamon, and salt. Set aside.
3. In a large bowl, cream the butter and sugar together. Add the pumpkin, Greek yogurt, and egg. Mix thoroughly.
4. Slowly add the flour mixture to the pumpkin combination. Mix well. Drop by rounded spoonfuls onto the baking sheets. Bake for 15 minutes until golden brown. Let cool on the pan for 5 minutes, then transfer to a wire rack to cool for another 5 minutes before frosting.

PER COOKIE, WITHOUT FROSTING

Calories: 74	Sugar: 3 g
Fat: 3 g	Fiber: 1 g
Cholesterol: 12 mg	Sodium: 51 mg
Carbohydrates: 10 g	Protein: 2 g

Cinnamon Yogurt Frosting

This light frosting can go with any of your sweet baked goods. Refrigerating is necessary for this frosting to thicken and for the flavors to deepen.

 YIELDS 1 CUP

Ingredients

2 tablespoons butter, softened (not melted)

¼ cup nonfat vanilla Greek yogurt

¼ teaspoon lemon juice

1 teaspoon ground cinnamon

1½ cups powdered sugar

PER TEASPOON

Calories: 20	Sugar: 4 g
Fat: 1 g	Fiber: 0 g
Cholesterol: 1.3 mg	Sodium: 4 mg
Carbohydrates: 4 g	Protein: 0.125 g

In a medium bowl, combine all the ingredients except powdered sugar and mix well. Slowly add the powdered sugar and mix with an electric mixer until smooth. Place in the refrigerator for 20 minutes to thicken.

LEMONY COOKIE BARS

These lemon bars are a perfect alternative to plain sugar cookies. They are not too sweet, and have just the right amount of lemon. Definitely use fresh lemons for this recipe!

 YIELDS 3 DOZEN BARS

Ingredients

1½ plus ¼ cups all-purpose flour, divided use

⅓ plus 1½ cups powdered sugar, divided use

¾ teaspoon salt, divided use

¾ cup butter, cold and sliced in pieces

3 eggs

¼ cup fresh lemon juice

½ cup nonfat plain Greek yogurt

½ teaspoon baking powder

2 teaspoons lemon zest

Extra powdered sugar, for sprinkling

PER BAR

Calories: 90	Sugar: 6 g
Fat: 4.5 g	Fiber: 0 g
Cholesterol: 28 mg	Sodium: 98 mg
Carbohydrates: 11 g	Protein: 1.5 g

1. Preheat the oven to 350°F. Grease a 9" × 13" baking dish and set aside.
2. In a large bowl, mix 1½ cups flour, ⅓ cup powdered sugar, and ½ teaspoon salt. Add sliced butter and mix well until crumbly. Pour the mixture into the prepared baking dish and pat down to form crust. Bake for 12–14 minutes until the edges are golden brown.
3. While the crust is baking, mix ¼ cup flour, 1½ cups powdered sugar, ¼ teaspoon salt, eggs, lemon juice, Greek yogurt, baking powder, and lemon zest in a large bowl with a mixer. Beat until smooth. Pour the lemon mixture on top of the hot cookie crust and return to oven. Bake for 35 minutes, until the topping is set and edges are light brown. Cool thoroughly in the pan. Sprinkle with extra powdered sugar, if desired, before serving. To store, cover and refrigerate for 3–5 days.

Selecting Quality Lemons

When buying lemons, make sure they are bright yellow and feel heavy. Lemons that feel light won't be very juicy. Also, always keep your lemons at room temperature. Refrigerated lemons won't produce as much juice. If you only have a lemon that isn't juicy yet, you can microwave it for 10–15 seconds to get the juices stimulated.

Dark Chocolate Cake

This moist cake will be a favorite recipe for years to come. With less butter, no oil, and added protein from the Greek yogurt, it's a healthier option than traditional cakes. Try frosting it with Deep Chocolate Frosting (see recipe in this chapter).

V SERVES 16

Ingredients
½ cup unsweetened dark cocoa

1½ cups all-purpose flour

1½ teaspoons baking soda

½ teaspoon instant coffee granules

1 cup turbinado sugar

1½ cups nonfat vanilla Greek yogurt

¼ cup butter, melted

4 eggs

1 teaspoon pure vanilla extract

2 tablespoons water

PER SERVING

Calories: 171	Sugar: 16 g
Fat: 5 g	Fiber: 1.2 g
Cholesterol: 60 mg	Sodium: 191 mg
Carbohydrates: 27 g	Protein: 5.5 g

1. Preheat the oven to 350°F. Grease 2 (8") cake pans.
2. In a medium bowl, stir together the cocoa, flour, baking soda, coffee, and sugar.
3. In a separate medium bowl, mix the Greek yogurt, melted butter, eggs, vanilla, and water until completely combined. Add the butter mixture to the flour combination, and beat for 3–4 minutes until smooth. Pour into the prepared cake pans.
4. Bake for 40 minutes, or until a toothpick placed in the center of the cakes comes out clean. Allow to cool completely before frosting.

Dark Chocolate for Better Health

When choosing chocolate, dark chocolate is the better choice. Dark chocolate may actually have health benefits. Studies show that eating dark chocolate a few times a week may help lower blood pressure and help control blood sugar. It is also filled with antioxidants, vitamins, and minerals. Look for dark chocolate with the highest content of cacao, preferably at least 70 percent. What a great excuse to eat some dark chocolate!

DEEP CHOCOLATE FROSTING

This frosting is light and fluffy, and can be used for many different cakes and cookies. The coffee enhances the flavor of the cocoa powder, which creates an incredibly intense chocolate taste and heavenly aroma.

 YIELDS 2 CUPS

Ingredients

6 tablespoons unsweetened dark cocoa powder

¼ teaspoon salt

1¾ cups powdered sugar

½ teaspoon instant coffee granules

2 tablespoons butter, melted and cooled

½ cup nonfat vanilla Greek yogurt

1 teaspoon pure vanilla extract

1. In a medium bowl, mix the cocoa powder, salt, sugar, and coffee. Set aside.
2. In a small bowl, combine the melted butter, Greek yogurt, and vanilla. Mix well. Add the Greek yogurt mixture to the cocoa mixture slowly, beating for 3–4 minutes until a creamy consistency is reached.

PER TABLESPOON

Calories: 37	Sugar: 7 g
Fat: 1 g	Fiber: 0.5 g
Cholesterol: 2 mg	Sodium: 25 mg
Carbohydrates: 7.5 g	Protein: 0.5 g

Almond Apple Bread Pudding

Your house will smell wonderful while this bread pudding is baking. This would go perfectly with a scoop of Vanilla Bean Frozen Yogurt (see recipe in this chapter).

Ⓥ SERVES 8

Ingredients

2 tablespoons butter

2 cups peeled and cubed Granny Smith apples

¼ cup raisins

3 tablespoons slivered almonds, divided use

¼ cup low-fat plain Greek yogurt

¾ cup fat-free milk

1 egg

1 teaspoon ground cinnamon

1 teaspoon pure vanilla extract

¼ teaspoon pumpkin pie spice

2 tablespoons brown sugar, packed

4 cups cubed bread

PER SERVING

Calories: 161	Sugar: 11 g
Fat: 6 g	Fiber: 2 g
Cholesterol: 35 mg	Sodium: 178 mg
Carbohydrates: 22 g	Protein: 4.75 g

1. Preheat the oven to 350°F. Grease a 9" × 9" baking dish.
2. In a large skillet, melt the butter. Cook the apples, raisins, and 2 tablespoons almonds over medium-low heat for 3–4 minutes until the apples are soft and the raisins have plumped. Remove from heat and set aside.
3. In a large bowl, add the Greek yogurt, milk, egg, cinnamon, vanilla, pumpkin pie spice, and brown sugar and beat with electric mixer until well blended. Add the apple mixture and stir to combine. Add the bread cubes, and mix to make sure all cubes are coated. Pour the mixture into the prepared baking dish. Bake for 40–45 minutes until the middle is set and edges are golden brown. Let cool for 5 minutes. Top with the remaining almonds and serve with frozen Greek yogurt, if desired.

CHOCOLATE CHIP COOKIES

These cake-like cookies will satisfy even the biggest critics of Greek yogurt. These are healthier than your typical cookie, although they taste sinfully delicious. You could also try substituting dried fruits or nuts for the chocolate chips!

 YIELDS 4 DOZEN

Ingredients

1 cup whole-wheat flour
1½ cups all-purpose flour
½ cup ground flaxseed
1 teaspoon baking powder
1 teaspoon baking soda
½ teaspoon salt
½ teaspoon ground cinnamon
½ cup butter, at room temperature
1 cup brown sugar
¼ cup turbinado sugar
½ cup unsweetened applesauce
½ cup nonfat vanilla Greek yogurt
1 teaspoon pure vanilla extract
1 egg
1 cup semi-sweet chocolate chips

1. Preheat the oven to 350°F.
2. In a medium bowl, combine the flours, flaxseed, baking powder, baking soda, salt, and cinnamon. Mix well and set aside.
3. In another medium bowl, cream the butter and sugars together until smooth. Add the applesauce, Greek yogurt, vanilla, and egg. Mix well.
4. Add the flour mixture 1 cup at a time to the Greek yogurt combination. Mix until combined; be careful not to overmix.
5. Fold in the chocolate chips. Drop by rounded teaspoonfuls onto an ungreased nonstick baking tray.
6. Bake for 12–15 minutes until the tops are golden brown. Cool on the tray for 5 minutes before moving to a wire rack to cool completely.

PER COOKIE

Calories: 97	Sugar: 9 g
Fat: 4 g	Fiber: 1 g
Cholesterol: 10 mg	Sodium: 81 mg
Carbohydrates: 14.5 g	Protein: 1.5 g

VANILLA BEAN FROZEN YOGURT

This can be made with or without an ice cream maker. This recipe is so delicious, you'll never want to eat store-bought frozen yogurt—with all those unnecessary additives—again! If you don't have a vanilla bean, you can substitute 2 teaspoons pure vanilla extract.

 SERVES 6

Ingredients

2 cups low-fat plain Greek yogurt
1 vanilla bean, halved and scraped
2 tablespoons honey
½ cup powdered sugar

PER SERVING

Calories: 118
Fat: 1.5 g
Cholesterol: 4.5 mg
Carbohydrates: 19 g
Sugar: 13 g
Fiber: 0 g
Sodium: 32 mg
Protein: 7.5 g

1. Place all ingredients in a large bowl and mix well.
2. If using an ice cream maker, freeze according to the manufacturer's instructions. To store, spoon the frozen yogurt into a tall, upright plastic container, and place in the freezer.
3. If you're churning by hand, transfer the mixture to a shallow freezer-safe container with a lid. Seal tightly and place in the freezer for 30 minutes. Take out the container and stir the mixture with a fork, and place back in the freezer until solid. Repeat this process every 30 minutes or so, stirring vigorously to break up the ice crystals, until the yogurt is well frozen. Allow to sit at room temperature for 5 minutes before serving. Store in an airtight container for up to 2 weeks.

Spice Up Your Yogurt

Get creative with your frozen yogurt! Feel free to add chocolate chips, crushed pretzels, crushed cookies, or other treats. You can add them right before serving, or you can stir them in and refreeze for 15 minutes.

WHITE CHOCOLATE CHIP BROWNIES

Greek yogurt replaces the oil found in traditional brownie recipes, and gives these brownies a soft, cake-like texture. Chocolate brownies with white chocolate chips are a delicious combination, and look delightful.

Ⓥ SERVES 16

Ingredients
½ cup butter, melted
¾ cup turbinado sugar
2 eggs
1 teaspoon pure vanilla extract
⅓ cup unsweetened cocoa powder
¾ cup all-purpose flour
¼ teaspoon salt
¼ teaspoon baking powder
½ cup nonfat plain Greek yogurt
¾ cup white chocolate chips

PER SERVING

Calories: 187	Sugar: 16 g
Fat: 10 g	Fiber: 0.75 g
Cholesterol: 42 mg	Sodium: 120 mg
Carbohydrates: 23 g	Protein: 2.5 g

1. Preheat the oven to 350°F. Grease an 8" square baking pan with organic nonstick cooking spray.
2. In a medium bowl, mix the butter, sugar, eggs, and vanilla until well blended. In a smaller bowl, combine the cocoa, flour, salt, and baking powder.
3. Slowly add the flour mixture to the butter mixture and stir. Add the Greek yogurt and stir until just combined, being careful not to overmix. Fold in the chocolate chips.
4. Pour the batter into the prepared pan and bake for 30 minutes, or until a toothpick placed in the center comes out clean. Cool completely in the pan before cutting and serving.

PISTACHIO COOKIES

There's no need to tell the kids that the secret ingredient in these cookies is avocado. These are light and sweet with a wonderful texture.

 YIELDS 4 DOZEN

Ingredients

1 cup whole-wheat flour
1½ cups all-purpose flour
½ cup ground flaxseed
1 teaspoon baking powder
1 teaspoon baking soda
½ teaspoon salt
½ teaspoon ground cinnamon
½ cup butter, at room temperature
½ cup ripe avocado, mashed
1 cup brown sugar
¼ cup turbinado sugar
½ cup nonfat plain Greek yogurt
1 teaspoon pure vanilla extract
1 egg
1¾ cups chopped pistachios

PER COOKIE

Calories: 100
Fat: 5 g
Cholesterol: 10 mg
Carbohydrates: 12 g

Sugar: 6 g
Fiber: 1 g
Sodium: 81 mg
Protein: 2 g

1. Preheat the oven to 350°F.
2. In a medium bowl, combine the flours, flaxseed, baking powder, baking soda, salt, and cinnamon. Mix well and set aside.
3. In another medium bowl, cream the butter, avocado, and sugars together until smooth. Add the Greek yogurt, vanilla, and egg. Mix well.
4. Add the flour mixture 1 cup at a time to the Greek yogurt combination. Mix until combined; do not overmix.
5. Fold in the pistachios. Drop by rounded teaspoonfuls onto an ungreased nonstick baking tray.
6. Bake for 12–15 minutes until the tops are golden brown. Cool on the tray for 5 minutes before moving to a wire rack to cool completely.

A Healthy Substitute for Butter

Don't let the green color scare you! Avocado makes a wonderful substitute for butter. Its creamy texture creates light, cake-like cookies. Avocados are loaded with heart-healthy unsaturated fats, vitamins, minerals, fiber, and protein. The part of the avocado that is closest to the skin is the most packed with nutrients, so be sure to scrape the insides to take advantage of these nutritional benefits.

CARROT CAKE

This moist, delicious cake is made lighter by adding Greek yogurt and using less oil and sugar. Crushed pineapple may seem like an odd ingredient in carrot cake, but you can't taste the pineapple; it simply adds sweetness and moisture. Try frosting this cake with Cream Cheese Yogurt Frosting (see recipe in this chapter).

 SERVES 16

Ingredients

All-purpose flour, for coating pan
2 cups whole-wheat pastry flour
2 teaspoons baking powder
1½ teaspoons baking soda
2 teaspoons ground cinnamon
¼ teaspoon salt
2 teaspoons pure vanilla extract
3 eggs, beaten
¾ cup turbinado sugar
¾ cup brown sugar
½ cup grapeseed oil
½ cup applesauce, unsweetened
½ cup low-fat plain Greek yogurt
1 (20-ounce) can crushed pineapple, drained
2 cups shredded carrots
½ cup chopped walnuts (optional)
½ cup raisins (optional)

PER PIECE, WITHOUT FROSTING

Calories: 281	Sugar: 27 g
Fat: 11 g	Fiber: 4 g
Cholesterol: 40 mg	Sodium: 264 mg
Carbohydrates: 42.5 g	Protein: 5 g

1. Preheat the oven to 350°F and position the oven rack in the center of the oven. Grease a Bundt pan and coat with all-purpose flour.
2. In a medium bowl, mix together the whole-wheat flour, baking powder, baking soda, cinnamon, and salt. Stir until mixed.
3. In another medium bowl, mix together the vanilla, eggs, sugars, oil, applesauce, and Greek yogurt until thoroughly combined.
4. Gradually fold in the flour mixture into the egg mixture while continuing to stir. Mix until everything is combined. Fold in the pineapple, carrots, and walnuts and raisins, if using. Stir to combine.
5. Pour into the prepared pan and bake for 40–45 minutes, until a toothpick inserted in the cake's center comes out clean. Allow to cool completely on a wire rack before frosting.

All about Grapeseed Oil

Grapeseed oil is an oil created by pressing the seeds of grapes. It has a very mild, clean taste and can be used in many different recipes. It has a high smoke point (higher than olive oil, corn, or sesame), which means it is preferable for frying. Grapeseed oil is packed with healthy essential fatty acids, vitamins, minerals, and antioxidants.

CREAM CHEESE YOGURT FROSTING

This delectable frosting is perfect for a variety of cakes and cookies. It can be stored in the refrigerator in an airtight container for up to 5 days.

 YIELDS 2½ CUPS FROSTING

Ingredients

2 tablespoons butter, softened

½ cup nonfat plain Greek yogurt

½ cup cream cheese, softened

1 teaspoon pure vanilla extract

1½ cups powdered sugar

In a medium bowl, mix together the butter, Greek yogurt, cream cheese, and vanilla. Gradually stir in the powdered sugar, and beat until thoroughly mixed. Refrigerate for at least 30 minutes to thicken before using.

PER TABLESPOON

Calories: 31	Sugar: 5 g
Fat: 1 g	Fiber: 0 g
Cholesterol: 3 mg	Sodium: 21 mg
Carbohydrates: 5 g	Protein: 0.6 g

PERFECT GLUTEN-FREE PUMPKIN PIE WITH PECAN CRUST

This pie can be enjoyed any time of year—not just during the holidays! It even goes perfectly with an afternoon cup of tea. The entire pie is gluten- and wheat-free.

 SERVES 8

Ingredients

Crust

¾ cup pecans

1 cup blanched almond flour

⅛ teaspoon salt

¼ teaspoon baking soda

½ teaspoon ground cinnamon

½ teaspoon pumpkin pie spice (cinnamon, ginger, allspice, and nutmeg)

1 teaspoon gluten-free vanilla extract

4 tablespoons coconut oil (or cold butter)

3 tablespoons 100 percent pure maple syrup

1 egg

Pie

1 (15-ounce) can pure pumpkin (not pumpkin pie filling)

½ cup low-fat milk

¼ cup nonfat plain Greek yogurt

2 eggs

2 teaspoons cinnamon

½ teaspoon ground ginger

1. Preheat the oven to 350°F.
2. Place the pecans in a food processor and process until you have a coarse flour.
3. Add the almond flour, salt, baking soda, cinnamon, pumpkin pie spice, vanilla, coconut oil, maple syrup, and egg, and pulse until a ball of dough forms.
4. Using the palms of your hands, press the dough into the bottom and up the sides of a 9" pie pan. Spread into a thin layer throughout the sides and bottom. Bake for 10 minutes.
5. Place all ingredients for the pie in a medium bowl and mix thoroughly. Pour the batter into the pie pan and bake for 60 minutes, or until toothpick placed in the center comes out clean. Allow to cool for 5 minutes before serving.

PER SERVING

Calories: 386

Fat: 25 g

Cholesterol: 81 mg

Carbohydrates: 38 g

Sugar: 26 g

Fiber: 6 g

Sodium: 158 mg

Protein: 8.5 g

Standard U.S./Metric Measurement Conversions

VOLUME CONVERSIONS

U.S. Volume Measure	Metric Equivalent
⅛ teaspoon	0.5 milliliter
¼ teaspoon	1 milliliter
½ teaspoon	2 milliliters
1 teaspoon	5 milliliters
½ tablespoon	7 milliliters
1 tablespoon (3 teaspoons)	15 milliliters
2 tablespoons (1 fluid ounce)	30 milliliters
¼ cup (4 tablespoons)	60 milliliters
⅓ cup	90 milliliters
½ cup (4 fluid ounces)	125 milliliters
⅔ cup	160 milliliters
¾ cup (6 fluid ounces)	180 milliliters
1 cup (16 tablespoons)	250 milliliters
1 pint (2 cups)	500 milliliters
1 quart (4 cups)	1 liter (about)

WEIGHT CONVERSIONS

U.S. Weight Measure	Metric Equivalent
½ ounce	15 grams
1 ounce	30 grams
2 ounces	60 grams
3 ounces	85 grams
¼ pound (4 ounces)	115 grams
½ pound (8 ounces)	225 grams
¾ pound (12 ounces)	340 grams
1 pound (16 ounces)	454 grams

OVEN TEMPERATURE CONVERSIONS

Degrees Fahrenheit	Degrees Celsius
200 degrees F	95 degrees C
250 degrees F	120 degrees C
275 degrees F	135 degrees C
300 degrees F	150 degrees C
325 degrees F	160 degrees C
350 degrees F	180 degrees C
375 degrees F	190 degrees C
400 degrees F	205 degrees C
425 degrees F	220 degrees C
450 degrees F	230 degrees C

BAKING PAN SIZES

U.S.	Metric
8 × 1½ inch round baking pan	20 × 4 cm cake tin
9 × 1½ inch round baking pan	23 × 3.5 cm cake tin
11 × 7 × 1½ inch baking pan	28 × 18 × 4 cm baking tin
13 × 9 × 2 inch baking pan	30 × 20 × 5 cm baking tin
2 quart rectangular baking dish	30 × 20 × 3 cm baking tin
15 × 10 × 2 inch baking pan	30 × 25 × 2 cm baking tin (Swiss roll tin)
9 inch pie plate	22 × 4 or 23 × 4 cm pie plate
7 or 8 inch springform pan	18 or 20 cm springform or loose bottom cake tin
9 × 5 × 3 inch loaf pan	23 × 13 × 7 cm or 2 lb narrow loaf or pâté tin
1½ quart casserole	1.5 liter casserole
2 quart casserole	2 liter casserole

INDEX

About the Author

Lauren Kelly is a certified nutritionist, recipe developer, Skinnygirl Cocktails Insider, food blogger, and the staff nutritionist at The Bar Method in Montclair, New Jersey, where she offers nutrition workshops and individualized counseling. She is also the author of *The Everything® Wheat-Free Diet Cookbook*. She has been featured in *Shape* magazine, the *Alternative Press*, and on Giuliana Rancic's website, FabFitFun.com. You can visit Lauren's website at LaurenKellyNutrition.com.